The Monarchy of France

THE
MONARCHY
OF FRANCE

CLAUDE DE SEYSSEL

TRANSLATED BY
J. H. HEXTER

EDITED, ANNOTATED, AND INTRODUCED BY
DONALD R. KELLEY

ADDITIONAL TRANSLATIONS BY
MICHAEL SHERMAN

New Haven and London
Yale University Press

Published with assistance from the foundation
established in memory of Philip Hamilton McMillan
of the Class of 1894, Yale College

Designed by James J. Johnson
and set in VIP Palatino type.
Printed in the United States of America by
Edwards Brothers Inc., Ann Arbor, Mich.

Library of Congress Cataloging in Publication Data

Seyssel, Claude de, 1450?–1520.
  The monarchy of France.

  Translation of La monarchie de France et deux autres
fragments politiques.
  Includes index.
  1. France—Politics and government—1328–1589.
2. Monarchy. I. Kelley, Donald R. II. Title.
JN2341.S413   321.6′0944   80–23554
ISBN 0–300–02516–5

10 9 8 7 6 5 4 3 2 1

To the memory of
CHARLES HOWARD MCILWAIN
and
GARRETT MATTINGLY
from
two of their deeply indebted students

Contents

Introduction

Modern political consciousness was born in the first phase of the Italian wars precipitated by the French invasion of 1494. This is an old story, enshrined in the classic work of nineteenth-century scientific historiography and perhaps not much attended to in this age of social and economic preoccupations and of "uneventful history." Yet it is not a phenomenon that academic fashion can obliterate. In the early sixteenth century it was not economic distress or social turmoil that had the most shocking and shaping impact on conceptions of the human condition and indeed on rational thought in general. In the new proto-journalistic medium of print the headline stories concerned not the price revolution, the rising middle class, or even (yet) religious scandal but rather the heroic efforts of warfare and the grandiose designs of diplomacy—the public repercussions of the ways of the lion and the fox.

It was, in short, the age of Machiavelli, a time when modern warfare and statecraft came, at least for a time, to dominate public opinion. It was also, of course, the age of Erasmus, and the attendant pacifist and universalist ideals likewise informed the vision of politics on the eve of the Reformation. This vision, alternately predatory and utopian, was created by an incomparable constellation of men of genius who, constituting what might be identified as the generation of 1494, witnessed and helped to bring about the

birth of what used to be called the modern world.[1] Within
the space of a half-dozen years there appeared as many classic books reflecting different aspects of modern political consciousness: Machiavelli's *Prince* (1513), Castiglione's *Courtier*
(1516), Erasmus's *Education of a Christian Prince* (1516),
Thomas More's *Utopia* (1516), Guillaume Budé's *Institution of
the Prince* (1519), and Claude de Seyssel's *Monarchy of France*
(1515).[2] In these works we can see the confluence of numerous currents but above all the basic ingredients of political
thought: the conceptualizations of antiquity, the values and
assumptions of medieval Christendom, and the predica-
ments of modern society.

Claude de Seyssel is still perhaps the least known of these
men of '94, yet in many ways his political vision was the
broadest and most sensitive to the realities of his age. He is a
pivotal figure in the history of political and social thought,
suggesting ties and inviting comparisons with a variety of
authors and traditions. Medieval jurisprudence, Gallican
ecclesiology, Aristotelian political science, the new "Italian-
style" diplomacy, the conventional mirror-of-prince and
art-of-war genres, and the emerging fields of institutional
history and social analysis—all these elements may be de-
tected in his work and especially in the crowning achievement of his literary career, the book on the "grand
monarchy" presented to King Francis I in 1515.[3] To the

1. Historical and conceptual background is established by J. H. Hexter,
The Vision of Politics on the Eve of the Reformation (New York, 1973); Felix
Gilbert, *Machiavelli and Guicciardini* (Princeton, 1965); and Garrett Mattingly,
Renaissance Diplomacy (New York, 1955).

2. In general see Lester K. Born's introduction to Erasmus, *Education of
a Christian Prince* (New York, 1936); Allen H. Gilbert, *Machiavelli's "Prince"
and its Forerunners* (Durham, 1938); Wilhelm Berges, *Die Fürstenspiegel des
hohen und späten Mittelalters* (Stuttgart, 1952); and Claude Bontems et al., "Le
Prince" dans la France des XVIe et XVIIe siècles (Paris, 1965).

3. See the introduction of Jacques Poujol's edition of Claude de Seyssel,
La Monarchie de France (Paris, 1961) (hereafter cited as Poujol), and below, n.
51. Following Poujol we omit the "grand" from the title and use the simpler
form (presumably Seyssel's preference) in the manuscripts.

pre-Lutheran vision of politics Seyssel's contribution was conservative, eclectic, a bit complacent, and in various ways mediative between the idealism of Erasmus, More, and Budé and the perhaps exaggerated realism of Machiavelli, Guicciardini, and Commynes. He tried to bridge the gap not only between theory and practice, between philosophy and statecraft, but also between the intellectual form and substance of modern political science and the reality and potentiality of sixteenth-century society. Without neglecting either the ideals of More or the anti-ideals of Machiavelli, Seyssel at all points preserved the ties between political thought and historical context, and this effort gives his work a value not shared by many of its contemporary rivals. In trying to be a practical guide to sixteenth-century political action Seyssel's work provides a direct access to sixteenth-century political consciousness. But his work, particularly the *Monarchy*, was above all an expression of his life.

THE LIFE

Seyssel was born into an ancient and noble Savoyard family in 1450 or a little later.[4] He was the illegitimate son of another Claude de Seyssel (1427–?), who later became marshal of Savoy, and Guillerme de la Motte. For most of his life he was called "Monsieur d'Aix" since Aix was his original home (not Seyssel, a little town less than 10 kilometers north and about halfway on the road to Geneva). The Seyssel family was related to as well as aligned with the counts of Savoy and so was committed to the French party. This political legacy contributed directly to Seyssel's career and at least indirectly to the attitude reflected in his major work.

Seyssel's education was substantial, but he had little direct contact with classical humanism, nor did he even study rhetoric under his teacher Pierre Mercier de Chambéry.

4. The standard and exhaustive biography is Alberto Caviglia, *Claudio di Seyssel (1450–1520)* (Turin, 1928), with an appendix of documents.

His enthusiasm for antiquity, like Machiavelli's, stemmed largely from career needs and was peripheral to the concerns of the Italian scholarship that was becoming so fashionable among intellectuals. The substance of his learning was in fact legal. He studied civil law at the University of Turin with Jacques Michelet de Saint-Georges and at Pavia with the great Giason del Maino. In 1486 he took his doctorate at Turin and was immediately launched into a teaching career that continued at least intermittently for the next decade. It appears that Seyssel engaged in that pastime most popular among the university students, "the lovers of Turin," as they were called, for he had two illegitimate daughters by two different women in these years. But neither these incidents nor his own bastardly status seemed to interfere in any way with his career. As a teacher he was apparently popular and somewhat innovative, lecturing for a time extemporaneously until this practice was forbidden. Among his students were Domenico de San Germano, who later edited his legal commentaries, and the famous Barthélemy de Chasseneux.

But temperament as well as family tradition soon drew Seyssel into politics, and he never entirely extricated himself. From 1490 the French party, led by Seyssel's cousin Guy de Chambre, was at odds with the duke of Savoy, who inclined toward the Piedmontese party, and Seyssel may have found his residence in Turin somewhat uncomfortable. In any case, in 1492 he left for the court of France and soon entered into the service of King Charles VIII, patron of his party, who was even then making plans for his invasion of Italy. Except that he continued to represent the French party, Seyssel's role is not clear; for during these years when the Italian wars were in the making he also served as "counsellor" to Louis d'Orléans, the future Louis XII, and to the duke of Savoy. Obviously he contributed in at least a minor way to the great enterprise of Italy of 1494, and perhaps specifically to the taking of Asti, a task assigned to the duke of Orléans. In any case, professionally as well as intellectually, Seyssel was—with Commynes, Machiavelli, Guicciardini and others—drawn into the "new politics" that appeared in the crucible of the Italian wars.

In 1496 and 1498 Seyssel's political career took two turns for the better: first by the accession of Filippo di Brescia as duke of Savoy, since it resulted in a shift back to a French-oriented policy; and second by the accession of Louis d'Orléans to the French throne. As a result Seyssel became "private and perpetual councillor" to Savoy, and then one of twenty counsellors to the Great Council of Louis XII, as well as (in 1499) royal counsellor to the Parlement of Toulouse and, after the French king's reinvasion of Italy and defeat of the duke, Ludovico il Moro, to the Senate of Milan. Seyssel was capable of advising either military firmness, as when Ludovico made a last-ditch assault on Milan to recover it, or diplomatic moderation, as in the aftermath of that attack, when he opposed retaliation. In these advisory duties he was both building upon his familiarity with legal wisdom and working his way toward the more practical view of statesmanship that was displayed in his *Monarchy of France*—in which, appropriately enough, the problem of "counsel" occupied a central position.

For the remainder of his life Seyssel's career remained on a multitrack, Franco-Savoyard course. He was a pluralist on more than one career ladder. Besides being rector of the University of Turin, he accepted a benefice in Mondavi and later administered the diocese of Lodi, although not until 1503 did he obtain a dispensation to enter priestly orders in order to pursue an ecclesiastical career in proper fashion. At the same time he broadened his diplomatic experience through missions to the Emperor Maximilian, to Bologna, Pavia, and Venice, while he was able to put his legal training to use again in his work for Louis XII to obtain an annulment of his marriage with Queen Jeanne. He also had an opportunity to

attend a conclave in Rome in 1503 in the company of the cardinal of Amboise, though his principal work in these years
continued to be as the king's representative to and adminis-
trator of the Milanese. In 1506 he was given an important
diplomatic mission to England and later others to Bern. In-
creasingly, Seyssel spent time in France (whose language he
was finally perfecting), though in 1510 he accompanied Louis
XII to Italy for his campaign against Venice. After this he was
rewarded by an appointment to the bishopric of Marseille,
though he did not retire to this honor until 1515. Before that
came Seyssel's perhaps most significant mission. After fail-
ing to get diplomatic support from the emperor or the Swiss
in the attempt to end the schism between France and the Papacy, Seyssel went directly to Rome to negotiate with Pope
Leo X; and late in 1514, at the eighth session of the Lateran
Council, he sealed an agreement that led the way to the Concordat of 1515, which completed the formation of the national
church in France.[5]

The period of Seyssel's service to France corresponded
almost exactly with the reign of Louis XII and so with the
major phases of the Italian wars. It corresponded also with
the active political career of Machiavelli, who likewise divided his time between internal administrative and diplomatic assignments. Their common experience, common
Italian backgrounds, and common ideals (despite different
power bases) go far to explain the remarkable similarities
between their interests, perceptions, and in many cases conclusions. Both were fascinated with the problems of political
stability and change—with the sources of national strength
and potential for imperial expansion and especially with the
sort of "counsel" that would promote these as well as the
more elevated values and goals of a society. The major difference was that while Machiavelli concentrated on "policy" in

5. Ludwig Pastor, *The History of the Popes*, trans. R. F. Kerr (St. Louis,
1923), 7:66; cf. Jules Thomas, *Le Concordat de 1516* (Paris, 1910).

a conventional sense, Seyssel paid greater attention to specific cultural tradition, especially to organized religion and to "police" in the sense of existing laws and institutions. Hardly less important, at least on an emotional level, was the fact that Machiavelli was much more familiar with the experience of losing. His vision was formulated largely in the bitterness of enforced retirement after the failure of the government he had served. By contrast, Seyssel drew inspiration from various French victories, especially that over the Venetians in 1512 and that of Marignano achieved just after his own—most honorable and rewarded—retirement.

On 15 January 1515, exactly two weeks after the death of Louis XII, Seyssel resigned his office as *maître des rêquetes* in the Parlement of Paris[6] and during the next three months completed his *Monarchy*. On April 1 he arrived in Marseille to assume his episcopal charge, which he had actually received four years before. Drawn by his first allegiances, however, he made attempts, successful two years later, to be transferred to the archbishopric of Turin. In his last years he continued his dual career, acting as counsellor to Duke Charles II of Savoy as well as carrying on pastoral duties, most notably the pursuit of Waldensian heresy in his diocese. During this time he also revised his book and saw its publication in July 1519. These revisions reveal his growing involvement in the cause of religious reform in a general sense, confessing pastoral neglect and nonresidence to be his own "fault and error" as well as that of many others. He was also aware of the incipient conflict between Geneva and Savoy and the looming conflict over the imperial election, but his letters (the last dated 19 December 1519) do not suggest any sense of major crisis.[7] To him as to others of the

---

6. Roland Mousnier, *Le Conseil du roi de Louis XII à la révolution* (Paris, 1970), p. 47.

7. The Vienna manuscript (Haus, Hof- und Staatsarchiv, Belgica, Politisches Archiv, Repertorium DD.B, Fasz. 231, fols. 36–114) is not auto-

generation of '94, the emerging reformation movement remained largely unappreciated. Content in his vision of a society that was competitive and sometimes corrupt but fun-
damentally stable and manageable, Archbishop Claude de
Seyssel died on 31 May 1520 and was interred in the Cathe-
dral of Turin.

THE WORKS

The published works of Claude de Seyssel vary from techni-
cal Latin scholarship to vernacular propaganda, but they
show a certain coherence and design. Aside from diplomatic
correspondence and elderly ventures into theology, Seyssel
seldom wavered from his concern with problems of society
and government. First in point of time came his commentaries on civil and feudal law, which were based on lectures
given in the late 1480s and early '90s at the University of
Turin and published in 1508. Later, during the first decade of
the sixteenth century, came his exercises in royalist propaganda and his translations from ancient historians. In Seyssel's masterwork, *The Monarchy of France*, elements of all
these labors can be seen: the jurist's concern for laws and
institutions; the royal apologist's interest in defending and
celebrating the heritage of the French crown and its
triumphs; the expert diplomat's view of statecraft, interna-
tional relations, military as well as political, and counsel; and
the humanist's desire to ransack the past for examples and
models of behavior.

For Seyssel, jurisprudence was the highest form of

---

graph, but it includes Seyssel's marginal corrections (see pt. II, n. 21) that
made their way into the printed edition of 1519, which however differs from
it in minor respects. The provenance is not clear (except that it came from the
Netherlands in the Napoleonic period), nor its exact affiliation with the Bibliothèque Nationale manuscript that forms the basis of Poujol's edition,
though genealogically it stands somewhere between that and the printed
edition. See below, n. 51.

knowledge, and its practitioners were literally "priests of the law" (*sacerdotes legum*). Such were the claims made at the very outset of the Digest, that authoritative anthology of classical jurisprudence that constituted as well the basic textbook of legal study. "Jurisprudence is the true philosophy," he quoted, "and because of its purpose it is superior to all other sciences."[8] This purpose, he continued in an equally conventional formula, "consisted not in speculation but in action." So at the very beginning of his career Seyssel sounded the themes that were to dominate his political thinking and behavior: the supremacy of law and the overriding urgency of the *vita activa* and the union of theory and practice, of ancient learning and modern experience.

As a legal scholar Seyssel was very much the conservative, as he made clear in his praise of Bartolus (*laus Bartoli*), the fourteenth-century jurist most closely identified with scholastic jurisprudence, and in his discipleship to that contemporary "Bartolist," Giason del Maino (*mihi doctrina pater*).[9] He followed scholastic form in discussing conventional rubrics and scholastic method in collecting various opinions over two centuries with the intention of arriving at scholarly consensus (*communis opinio; concordia opinionum*). Seyssel was no legal humanist (unlike that younger disciple of Giason, Andrea Alciato), and yet he was by no means lacking in philological sophistication or a sense of the historical development of law. "Former scholars commented on the first part of the Digest in different styles and over various periods of time," he remarked; and more specifically he distinguished three phases of legal scholarship (*antiqui, noviores, modernique*), referring to the classical jurists, to the

8. Seyssel, *Commentaria in sex partes Digestorum et Codicis* (n.p. 1508), fol. I. An unpublished legal work of Seyssel is "Tractatus xii quaestionum in materia criminis lese maiestatis" (Bibliothèque Nationale, Collec. Dupuy, vol. 558, fols. 17–37). There is no study of Seyssel's early legal writings.

9. Seyssel, *Speculum feudorum* (Basel, 1566), p. 4.

thirteenth-century glossators, and lastly to the commentators of his own school.[10] He recognized, too, the differing attitudes of civilians, canonists, and feudists (*legistae, canonistae, feudistae*) and the problems of the conflict of laws arising from the multinational heritage of European society. As for the *jus feudisticum*, Seyssel, again showing more respect for historical sense than for legal authority, placed himself in that minority which held that "the material of feudal law was wholly unknown to ancient lawyers," and hence had no ties with the Roman tradition.[11]

For Seyssel, civil law represented not only a way of ordering society but also, especially in the Romano-Byzantine corpus assembled by Justinian in the sixth century, an archetype of unified monarchy. About the seminal first section of the Digest ("On Law and Justice") Seyssel remarked, "There is no more elegant introduction to this title than that made by the emperor"; and it was in just this prefatory edict that Justinian set down the principles of legislative sovereignty and imperial power, a pattern in many ways instructive for the "police" of the monarchy of France.[12] Not, of course, that Seyssel proposed to defend the authority of the "empire" of his own day, that Germanized rival of the French monarchy. On the contrary, following the professional assumptions of the "ultramontane" (and anti-imperial) school, he applied these principles to the French ruler, who was, according to a famous canonist (and also anti-imperial) formula, "emperor in his kingdom."[13] In this way Seyssel imported into his adopted nation both the ideological resources of Roman law and the public-spiritedness of the Roman citizen—*civis* being equivalent, he argued, to the

10. Ibid., p. 3.
11. See D. R. Kelley, "De Origine Feudorum: the Beginnings of an Historical Problem," *Speculum* 39 (1964): 207–28.
12. Seyssel, *Commentaria*, p. 1.
13. Seyssel, *Speculum feudorum*, p. 28.

modern *patriota*, and adding that "Fatherland is not determined only by origin" (*Patria non solum dicitur respectu originis*).[14] So he transferred to France his allegiance as well as his learning.

Yet Seyssel was never content to limit his perceptions and conclusions on textual authority. "Natural law is always just and equitable," he declared, "while civil law is sometimes inequitable."[15] In Bartolist fashion he systematically presented his analysis of laws in terms of the Aristotelian four causes and according to the standard of natural law. He did this even in the case of feudal law, those *Consuetudines Feudorum*, whose barbaric—"rustic and obscene"—style and lack of order he deplored and whose authority in France he of course denied.[16] In general terms, however, the sources of feudal law (*materia feudorum*) merited inclusion in moral philosophy (*Liber Feudalis supponitur Ethicae parti Philosophiae*) and in Aristotle's rationalist scheme.[17] As with all laws, the efficient cause was the sovereign (which in the case of the *Consuetudines Feudorum* was to say the emperors of the twelfth and thirteenth centuries, and ultimately God); the material cause was the texts of particular laws, constitutions, decisions, and customs; the formal cause was the arrangement into books and titles (unfortunately so much less rational than the civil law model); and the final cause was the goal of supplying precepts or examples, in effect vicarious experience, "so that feudal questions can better be resolved."

It was with an analogous purpose in mind—so that political questions can better be resolved—that Seyssel turned to the study of classical history. In the meantime he had abandoned the academy for a more active political

14. Seyssel, *Commentaria*, fol. III^v.
15. Ibid., fol. XXVI.
16. Seyssel, *Speculum feudorum*, p. 2.
17. Ibid., pp. 19, 11.

career, and the "vicarious experience" relevant to his new role had to be sought beyond the confines of jurisprudence. In 1504 Seyssel visited the royal library in Blois in the company of the great Hellenist Jean Lascaris, and the experience inspired a collaboration over the next few years that produced a series of pioneering translations from Greek historians into French.[18] Xenophon's *Anabasis* (via Lascaris's Latin) was presented to Louis XII in 1504 and to Charles II of Savoy a year later. This was followed in 1510 by translations of Justin's abridgement of Trogus Pompeius, of Diodorus Siculus (along with extracts from Plutarch), and in 1514 of Eusebius and Thucydides (from Lorenzo Valla's translation). For each translation Seyssel composed an introduction on some topic related to his work as a translator, the book in question, current events, and various intellectual issues. The translations, published posthumously, all left their mark on and added historical substance to *The Monarchy of France*. Among the prologues the ones for Justin and Appian are most illuminating and relevant for Seyssel's political views and attempts to join ancient wisdom to modern policy, and for this reason they have been appended in translation to the *Monarchy*.

Seyssel's translations also contributed to his secondary mission, which was cultivation of the vernacular to the further glory of "la nation françoise," as he told Louis XII in 1510.[19] Contact with humanist scholarship led Seyssel to an

18. See P. Chavy, "Les Traductions humanistes de Claude de Seyssel," in *L'Humanisme français au début de la Renaissance* (Paris, 1973), pp. 361–76, and Börje Knös, "Un Ambassadeur de l'hellénisme—Janus Lascaris—et la tradition greco-byzantine dans l'humanisme français" (Uppsala, 1945). See also Poujol, introduction, pp. 22–24, with further bibliography.

19. Seyssel, "Exordium" to translation of Justin, *Histoire* (Paris, 1559), ed. by Poujol from Bibliothèque Nationale, Manuscrits, Fonds français, 715, and translated below, appendix 1, and also "Prologue" to translation of Xenophon, *Histoire du voyage qui fit Cyrus* . . . (Paris, 1529). Cf. F. Brunot, "Un projet d'enrichir, magnifier et publier la langue française en 1509," *Revue d'histoire littéraire de la France* 1 (1894): 27–37, and Hans Modlmayr, *Die Anwendung Artikels und Zahlwortes bei Claude de Seyssel* (Kempten, 1886).

appreciation not only of law but also of "la licterature," by which he meant writing in general, without which civilization was impossible. Without written records there could be no social order, he argued: "without law, without police, without justice, the weak would be driven mad and oppressed by the strong, and the good attacked and afflicted by the bad." Without records, intelligent counsel and formulation of policy, too, would be impossible. Such was Seyssel's utilitarian yet humanizing view of literature. "And of this literature," he declared, "history is the most profitable."

In his historiographical enterprise, as in his legal studies, Seyssel had a philosophical goal in mind, which was to find some pattern in the "continual mutation" of human experience, and so some remedy for that irrationality which men call fortune. "If men do not understand causes and effects," he wrote in his preface to Diodorus Siculus, "it is only because the weakness of our understanding prevents us from fathoming the secrets of nature." [20] In the preface to his translation of Appian he associated the value of historical study more specifically with political philosophy, referring in particular to the famous debate in Herodotus over the three forms of government. His conclusion was that mixed government—"so reasonable and civilized [politique] that it is altogether free from tyranny"—was the best of all. [21] In this connection he went on to describe the institutional arrangement of the French monarchy in particular, including the royal council, the ordinances and system of justice, and the state of the nobility. At this point (1510) it is clear that Seyssel was already formulating the thoughts that would receive more elaborate expression in the *Monarchy*.

Political duties furnished Seyssel with another incentive

20. Seyssel, "Proheme" to translation of Diodorus Siculus (Paris, 1530).
21. Seyssel, "Proheme" to translation of Appian, *Des Gestes des Romains* (Paris, 1544), ed. by Poujol (pp. 77–87) from Bibliothèque Nationale, Manuscrits, Fonds français, vol. 713, and translated below, appendix 2.

for historical studies. In 1506 he was sent on a mission to England to consult with Henry VII about Louis XII's decision to marry his daughter Claude not (as previously planned) to the young Charles of Burgundy but to François de Valois, heir to the French throne; and on this occasion he delivered an oration in praise of Louis XII. The final product was a eulogistic biography that was later given additional historical context and published in French as well as Latin editions. In 1510 Seyssel published an even more apologetic piece celebrating the victory of the French over the Venetians in 1508.[22] These two works of propaganda reflect two aspects of Seyssel's experience as royal counsellor and, again, two dominant themes of the *Monarchy*—the dual method of diplomacy and its natural extension, war.

In effect the biography of Louis XII was a historical evaluation of French political tradition from the standpoint of the house of Orléans. From the historian Florus Seyssel took the conceit of the four ages and applied it to French dynastic history: infancy from the beginning (the legendary Pharamond) to Clovis; youth down to the end of the Merovingians; maturity under the Carolingians; and finally old age under the Capetians. The only monarch deserving comparison with his own master, Seyssel argued, was Charlemagne, who was likewise effective in the arts both of war and of peace. To these Charlemagne added an adeptness in learning (illustrated by the legend of the Carolingian foundation of the University of Paris) not shared by Louis XII, but on the other hand the current government was much superior in its system of justice. Seyssel also compared Louis

22. Seyssel, *Les louenges du Roy Louis XIIe de ce nom* (Paris, 1508) and *La Victoire du Roi contre les Venitiens* (Paris, 1510), on which see Poujol, introduction, pp. 20–22; Innocenzo Cervelli, *Machiavelli e la crisi dello stato veneziano* (Naples, 1974), chap. 7; and Michael Sherman, "Political Propaganda and Renaissance Culture: French Reactions to the League of Cambrai, 1509–1510," *Sixteenth Century Journal* 8 (1977): 97–128, and especially his "Selling of Louis XII" (Ph.D. diss., University of Chicago, 1975).

XII with the Emperor Trajan and praised him in similar terms as "father of his country" (*pater patriae; père du peuple*). In general, the superiority of Louis XII was based on five areas of achievement: the pacification of the people internally, the establishment of order through law (the famous triad of "religion, justice, and police"), financial relief (by lowering the *taille*), the restoration of military discipline, and foreign conquests.[23] Once again this argument prefigures several of the main themes of the *Monarchy*.

The last of these themes, that of military expansion, was underlined in 1510 by the French victory over the Venetians in the war of the League of Cambrai. In his celebration of this event Seyssel repeated his praises of Louis XII's government and concluded that his judgment of the strength and stability of the French monarchy had been confirmed by the great effort demanded by this victory. But to this argument he added another that would figure prominently in the *Monarchy*, namely, an appreciation of the Venetian republic. In pointing out the stability and admirable "police" of this aristocratic govenment (*gouverné par si grant sens et police*), Seyssel was not only contributing to the growing "myth of Venice" but also establishing a contemporary standard of comparison for a fuller assessment of monarchy—and indeed a further basis for a defense of the ancient idea of "mixed government."[24] But what Seyssel admired above all was the contribution of Venetian institutions to its imperial expansion (*convenables à conserver et agrandir ung empire*), which alone was a test of political "force." This, he would agree with Machiavelli, was "how the strength of all states should be measured."[25]

By 1510, then, it seems clear that Seyssel had laid the foundations of his own political thought. He had become familiar with the diplomatic "game at chess," with more

23. Seyssel, *Les louenges*, fol. 7ᵛ, and see below, pt. 1, chap. 8.
24. Seyssel, *La Victoire*, pt. 2 and see below, pt. 1, n. 5.
25. Machiavelli, *The Prince*, chap. 10.

forceful kinds of imperial expansion, and with the underly-
ing sources of political and social strength. Above all, he had
arrived at his conception of the three essential "bridles"
(*freins*) of monarchy, which were at the same time repos-
itories of this strength. At first hand he had become familiar
with the theory and practice of "justice" and with that mul-
tifaceted concept, "police," which involved social structure
as well as the enforcement of laws and the establishment of
policy in a modern sense. Only the third member of the governmental trinity, "religion," had been neglected. Of course
Seyssel had long been involved in the ecclesiastical politics
surrounding the Council of Pisa and leading up to the Concordat of Bologna in 1515, and from 1511 he was bishop of
Marseille. But he had not attended to the devotional aspect of
his priestly or episcopal charges, and it weighed on his conscience. His interest in religious reform, sponsored at that
time in France by Lefèvre d'Etaples, was reflected in a commentary on the Gospel of St. Luke that Seyssel published in
1514; but his newfound piety could not be satisfied until he
retired from political office.[26] Upon the death of Louis XII on
1 January 1515 Seyssel began to carry out his resolve. Before
taking up his ecclesiastical office, however, he decided to set
down in a systematic way what he had learned of public life
and the political world and join it to his more formal
scholarly and philosophic studies. The finished product he
would present to the new King, Francis I. In effect it would
be his political testament.

The "Monarchy"

Seyssel's masterwork was written in the spring of 1515.[27] Following the pattern of another recently retired statesman,

26. Cf. Poujol, introduction, pp. 25–27, and Caviglia, *Claudio di Seyssel*,
pp. 321–555.
27. On this work see J. H. Hexter, "Claude de Seyssel and Normal Politics in the Age of Machiavelli," in *Art, Science and History in the Renaissance*,

Seyssel tried to assemble his hard-won political wisdom and to offer it in the conventional form of a handbook of counsel for a prince. Like Machiavelli, Seyssel made a show of novelty in placing practice above theory and, though without the extreme claims that Machiavelli made for his "new route," in collecting examples from antiquity.[28] Like Machiavelli, too, he took a dim view of human nature—"corrupt, ambitious and greedy"—and a realistic view of the nature and necessity of war. Unlike Machiavelli, however, Seyssel had left office with honor, expectations, and faith in established institutions. His method was based not only on "political reason" and "authentic historical example" but also on "approved authority,"[29] and this included two traditions of which Machiavelli was largely innocent—professional jurisprudence and French kingship. Seyssel indeed placed major emphasis on the twin arts of diplomacy and war; but these topics are taken up in the last three of the five parts of the *Monarchy*, only after the social, legal, and institutional framework has been established in parts one and two—in contrast to Machiavelli's view of statecraft, which is often, perhaps too vulgarly, represented as politics without law. For Seyssel, politics might be represented as an extension of law (just as warfare was an extension of politics).

ed. Charles S. Singleton (Baltimore, 1967), pp. 389–415, and "Seyssel, Machiavelli and Polybius VI: the Mystery of the Missing Translation," *Studies in the Renaissance* 3 (1956): 75–96, as well as Hexter, *Vision of Politics*; William Church, *Constitutional Thought in Sixteenth Century France* (Cambridge, 1941), chap. 1; L. Gallet, "La Monarchie française d'après Claude de Seyssel," *Revue historique de droit français et étranger*, sér. 4, 23 (1944): 1–34; Wera Rahel Lewin, *Claude de Seyssel, Ein Beitrag zur politischen Ideengeschichte des 16. Jahrhunderts* (Heidelberg, 1933); John W. Allen, *A History of Political Thought in the Sixteenth Century* (London, 1928), pt. 3, chap. 2; and Roger Doucet, *Etude sur le gouvernement de François Ier dans ses rapports avec le Parlement de Paris* (Paris, 1921), 1:11–14. Most recent is the discussion of Quentin Skinner, *The Foundations of Modern Political Thought* (Cambridge, 1928), 2:26off.
    28. Machiavelli, *Discourses*, introduction.
    29. See below, Proem to *Monarchy*.

After arguing in philosophic and historical terms that monarchy was the best of the three Aristotelian forms, Seyssel proceeded to a discussion of the cycle of political change illustrated by the ancient Roman Empire and the contemporary Venetian republic. Then he settled down to his appraisal of the French monarchy in particular, drawing upon royalist ideology and mythology concerning the "mystical body" of the kingdom, the "Salic law" of masculine succession, and what would later be called the "fundamental laws" of the kingdom.[30] It was at this point that Seyssel introduced the notion of the three "bridles" on the "absolute" authority of the king derived from Roman law.[31] By "religion" he meant not only the force of Christian faith that made the French king "Most Christian" (*treschrestien*) and the Sorbonne the theological arbiter of Europe but the whole Gallican tradition that would—within the year and partly through Seyssel's own efforts—receive its classic royalist formulation in the Concordat of Bologna. By "justice" he referred not only to the ideals of jurisprudence and political philosophy in academic terms but also to the conventional processes of the French court system. Finally, by "polity" (*police*) he meant not only a theoretical constitutional structure but more specifically the legislative tradition of the French monarchy expressed in the royal ordinances (in principle going back to Carolingian times), which proposed governmental regulation and interference on every conceivable level of political, military, corporate, social, economic, and even domestic life. In general Seyssel presented a critical view of this institutional framework along two lines: descriptive, which is to say in

30. See J. R. Major, "The Renaissance Monarchy as seen by Erasmus, More, Seyssel and Machiavelli," *Action and Conviction in Early Modern Europe*, ed. Theodore K. Rabb and Jerrold Seigel (Princeton, 1969), pp. 17–31, and André Lemaire, *Les Lois fondamentales de la monarchie française d'après les théoriciens de l'ancien régime* (Paris, 1907).

31. See below, pt. 1, chaps. 8–11.

terms of French law and history as he had read and experienced them; and normative, which is to say in terms of the grand tradition of legal and (especially Aristotelian) political science. One of the main problems of his work is that he made so little effort to distinguish between the descriptive and the prescriptive modes—not to speak of the apologetic arguments that informed both.

The next stage of Seyssel's analysis introduced another and still more famous triad, the medieval notion of the three estates of the realm, along with attendant organismic conceptions of social harmony.[32] The apparent novelty of Seyssel's discussion stems from his Italian background. According to his view, the church does not represent a separate estate but is common to the other three, and these three are the nobility (robe as well as sword, according to later terminology), the middle (*moyen*) or rich (*gras*) people, and the lesser folk (*peuple menu*). The last two categories obviously correspond to what Machiavelli and many observers before him called the *popolo grasso* and *popolo minuto*, and the important thing is that they functioned as terms of social rather than legal analysis, designating classes rather than corporate groups. This same inclination toward proto-sociological argument can be seen in Seyssel's succeeding discussion of social mobility ("How men go from the third estate to the second and from the second to the first") and social coherence ("The harmony and agreement of the three estates").[33] Of course such analysis is carried on in the conventional terms of Aristotelian naturalism and medieval political—and social—theology (biological and mystical bodies), but this circumstance serves to underline the pivotal importance of Seyssel's contributions to Western social thought.

These traditional-innovative themes are presented in the first part of the *Monarchy*; in part two Seyssel moves on, as

32. See ibid., chaps. 13–16.
33. See ibid., chaps. 17–19.

promised, to more practical matters, namely, "The things necessary for the preservation and augmentation of the monarchy. . . ."[34] Here it is that the affinity with the mirror-of-princes genre (*De Regimine principum, Lunette des princes, Fürstenspiegel,* etc.) becomes evident, but it must be said that Seyssel is less interested in the classical protreptic style than in the modern problem of "counsel," both private and public, both informal and institutionalized. The model here is not only Seyssel himself but also, on a higher level, the role of such viceroyal counsellors as Louis XII's minister, Georges d'Amboise; and whether or not he was the original of "Let George do it," the proverb itself is in keeping with Seyssel's advice to the rash young Francis I. In this connection, in any case, Seyssel begins his survey of the particular councils and offices, lay and ecclesiastical, that were the vehicles of this "counsel" and the means of implementing "religion, justice, and police." One crucial problem concerned the policy that should be adopted toward the three estates; and following Aristotle's own counsel of moderation Seyssel warned against allowing the nobility to become either too "insolent" or too impoverished and against imposing excessive burdens on the "little people." As for the middling "fat people," Seyssel was led by the Aristotelian golden mean to advise a mercantilist and qualifiedly bullionist policy.[35] In every case the goal was enhancing the "grandeur" of the French monarchy and nourishing the natural imperialism that constituted its life-principle.

In this way Seyssel revealed the main thrust of the dynamic "new politics" of his age. In the three concluding sections of his book he discussed, in terms often similar to Machiavelli's *Art of War,* various aspects of military power—the life-principles of a "grand army," as it were, and

34. See below, pt. 2, passim.
35. See ibid., chap. 22.

the sustenance and "police" demanded by it.[36] Due attention was given to the new (and again largely Italianate) art of diplomacy, but, as always, no amount of political virtuosity could succeed without conspicuous military—and, Seyssel urged, thinking of the Venetian and English examples, *naval*—"force." So he concluded with an even more Machiavellian discussion of the ways to conquer "new states" (the abiding problem of the Italian wars) and how to preserve them through good "police."[37] Even for Seyssel, however, the "new politics" concealed the oldest of dreams, and he concluded his political testament with the pious hope that his wisdom would contribute not only to the honor of God and to the glory of the monarchy of France but also to "the recovery of the holy land." Questions of sincerity aside, Seyssel and Machiavelli were in conspicuous agreement about the social and strategic importance of joining piety and politics—a thesis that has appealed to many ages.

POST MORTEM

The *Monarchy*'s afterlife was by no means as colorful as that of *The Prince*, but its influence was considerable over the next two generations. A second edition appeared in 1541, a translation (though unpublished) was made into Italian, and in 1548 Johann Sleidan produced a partial rendering in Latin.[38] Seyssel would no doubt have writhed in his episcopal grave to know that he was "interpreted" by the official historiographer of the Lutheran party; but in terms of justice and police, if not religion, he would have agreed in many ways

36. See below, pts. 3 and 5.
37. See below, pt. 4.
38. *C. Seisselli . . . De Republica Galliae et Regum Officiis libri duo*, J. Sleidano, interprete (Strasbourg, 1548), and see P. Bourdon, " 'La grand Monarchie de France' de Claude de Seyssel et sa traduction en italien," Ecole française de Rome, *Mélanges d'archéologie et d'histoire* 28 (1908): 1–29, discussing a misattributed manuscript (Vatican, Urbinas 858).

with Sleidan's mistrust of the "tyranny" manifested by Charles V in his treatment of his subjects' "liberties." Although Sleidan inclined as much to resistance as to "constitutionalism," he very much appreciated Seyssel's political acumen in matters of diplomacy (in which Sleidan himself was expert) and the depth of his understanding of legal and institutional checks on government; appropriately Sleidan appended a translation from Plato's *Laws* to Seyssel's work.

In France the jurist Guillaume de la Perrière offered a *Miroir politique* (1555) that resembled the *Monarchy* in some respects, though it was both more idealized and more single-mindedly monarchist, denying that the parlements in any way "bridled" royal power.[39] Admiration for Seyssel's moral, juridical, and institutional interpretation of political "force" and behavior was especially apparent among Protestants, particularly French Huguenots, after the publication of the third edition of the *Monarchy* in 1557. The most notable example was the *Francogallia* of François Hotman, who contributed to constitutionalist mythology by a more historical consideration of the legal, conciliar, and parliamentary traditions of the French monarchy; but he was not alone.[40] Huguenot ideologists frequently celebrated the French estates in Seysselian terms; and one of them, Du Laurier, promoted his program of national reform on the basis of the secular trinity of "religion, justice, and police."[41] So, in a different way, did Innocent Gentillet, whose seminal *Discours contre Machiavel* (1579) refuted the alleged "atheism" and "tyranny" of Machiavelli in terms of the categories of "counsel" (instead of justice), "police," and religion.[42]

39. La Perrière, *Le Miroir politique* (Paris, 1555), Englished as *The Mirrour of Policie* (London, 1598).

40. Hotman, *Francogallia*, ed. R. E. Giesey and trans. J. H. M. Salmon (Cambridge, 1972).

41. Jean Du Laurier, *De l'Estat de ce royaume quant a la religion, justice et police* (Paris, 1583).

42. Gentillet, *Discours contre Machiavel*, ed. Antonio D'Andrea and Pamela D. Stewart (Florence, 1974).

Protestants were not the only ones to be attracted by Seyssel's ideas. In his pioneering *Recherches de la France* (which began appearing from 1560) Etienne Pasquier made use of the *Monarchy of France*, while the humanist Louis Le Roy turned to it extensively, and to the biography of Louis XII, not only in his translation of and commentary on Aristotle's *Politics* (1567) but also in his project, never carried through, to write a history of the French monarchy. "As in persons," Le Roy wrote, "there are naturally four ages in monarchies . . . , their beginning being comparable to infancy, early growth to adolescence, maturity to manhood, and decline to old age, dissolution, and death. The four ages of the [Roman] Empire have been distinguished by Seneca, Lancantius, and Florus; those of the kingdom of France by Seyssel in his panegyric of Louis XII; and those of England by Polydore Vergil."[43] The royal historiographer Bernard du Haillan worked this analysis out in detail, and indeed in largely Seyssellian terms, in his pioneering institutional history of the French monarchy published in 1570. Like Le Roy, Du Haillan also relied on Seyssel's class analysis, on his discussion of laws and customs and especially of the three "bridles" of monarchical power, and on his celebration of "mixed government," which became such a controversial issue during the civil wars. Similar borrowings are apparent in the historical survey of the French monarchy published in 1579 by François de Belleforest, who was not only Du Haillan's successor in the office of *historiographe du roi* but one of Hotman's severest critics.[44] In general, Seyssel's view of the French polity was compatible not only with conventional Gallicanism but also with the more exaggerated constitutionalism of the Hu-

43. Le Roy, *Les Monarchiques*, printed with his *Exhortation aux François pour vivre en concorde* (Paris, 1570); Pasquier, *Les Recherches de la France* (Paris, 1633), p. 682, e.g.; and cf. Poujol, appendix 1.

44. Du Haillan, *De l'Estat et succes des affaires de France* (Paris, 1570), and Belleforest, *Grandes Annales et Histoire Generale de France* (Paris, 1579), fol. 1ff; and cf. Poujol, appendix 2.

guenot party. By the last part of the sixteenth century it had become absorbed into both historiographical perspective and the political ideology of the "grand monarchy" of France.

Modern historical interest in Seyssel stems in general from the rediscovery of sixteenth-century France by historians of Restoration France, not only major figures like Thierry, Michelet, and Guizot, but also dozens of antiquarians and jurists drawn to the literary and legal traditions of the old regime. One example is the anti-Bonapartist pamphlet by J. E. D. Bernardi, lamenting (in 1814) the previous "twenty-five years without law," and referring for support to Seyssel as well as Montesquieu and Burke.[45] Seyssel benefited from this enterprise of national self-examination, but he did not receive serious treatment until the establishment of "scientific" history in the later nineteenth century. In 1892 he was the subject of a Latin dissertation at the University of Paris, and his work was placed in the context of early modern political thought in the pioneering work of Georges Weill.[46] Three years later a more popular article presented him to the reading public of France as a prominent expression of "national sentiment" and of awareness of "the ascendant march of the bourgeoisie," and in 1907 André Lemaire included Seyssel in a broad survey of the "fundamental laws" of the old regime, in which Seyssel is assigned to the school of "political traditionalism."[47]

In this century Seyssel has received more cosmopolitan and more critical treatment, beginning especially with his inclusion in Emile Picot's studies of sixteenth-century

45. Bernardi, *Observations sur l'ancienne constitution française* (Paris, 1814), published anonymously (Bibliothèque Nationale, Lb[45].164).

46. Charles Dufayard, "De Claudii Seisselli . . . vita et operibus" (Paris, 1892), and Weill, *Les Théories sur le pouvoir royal en France pendant les guerres de religion* (Paris, 1891), p. 14.

47. A. Jacquet, "Le Sentiment national au XVIe siècle, Claude de Seyssel," *Revue des questions historiques* 57 (1895): 400–40; and see above, n. 30.

"Italianized Frenchmen," and culminating in 1928 in the monumental biography by Alberto Caviglia (who unfortunately never carried out his plan of devoting a second volume to Seyssel's writings).[48] Five years later a German study by Wera Rahel Lewin appeared, emphasizing his "imperialism" as well as his "nationalism" and the medieval organismic terms that suggested a conception of a Renaissance *Rechtsstaat*, and during the second world war a valuable study of the *Monarchy* by Leon Gallet. In English, J. W. Allen published a brief appreciation in his survey of sixteenth-century political thought.[49] The most influential analysis, however, was probably the work of William Church, who carried the interests and attitudes of the great constitutional historian C. H. McIlwain across the Channel into the field of French "constitutional thought"; like Lemaire, Church stressed Seyssel's concern with the "fundamental laws" of the French monarchy, and, like Lewin, the organismic and "corporatist" direction of his thought. With similar encouragement from McIlwain, J. H. Hexter began investigating Seyssel and produced a number of ground-breaking articles as well as the present translation.[50] The most important of all contributions, aside from that of Caviglia, has been the edition of the *Monarchy* by Jacques Poujol, published with other materials and a critical introduction in 1961.[51]

48. Picot, *Les Français italianisants au XVIe siècle* (Paris, 1906), vol. I, chap. 1; and see above, n. 4.

49. See above, n. 27.

50. Ibid.

51. Claude de Seyssel, *La Monarchie de France et Deux autres Fragments*, ed. Jacques Poujol (Librairie d'Agences: Paris, 1961), based on Bibliothèque Nationale, Manuscrits, Fonds français, 5212 (but not the Vienna MS), with variations from the three editions: (1) *La Grant Monarchie de France* composée par messire Claude de Seyssel, lors evesque de Marseille et a present Archevesque de Thurin adressant au roy tres chrestien Françoys premier de ce nom (Regnault-Chaudiere: Paris, 1519); (2) *La grand monarchie de France* . . . (Galliot du Pré: Paris, 1541), along with *La loi Salicque* (see below, pt. I, n. 13); and (3) *La Grand Monarchie de France* . . . (Galliot du Pré: Paris, 1557), also with *La loi Salicque*.

The Translation (note by J. H. Hexter)

The translator of Claude Seyssel's *La Monarchie de France* turned it into English in the winter of 1946–47. At the time, he intended to prepare a historical introduction to it. For reasons both complex and uninteresting, he never got around to doing so. He is naturally delighted that Donald Kelley has admirably done the work that he himself neglected.

The translation was initially prepared from a photocopy of the first printed edition of the work. In 1950 the translator had the opportunity to examine the presentation manuscript of *La Monarchie,* which Seyssel dedicated to Francis I in 1515, and to check and modify the translation accordingly. The revised translation underwent a similar comparison with Jacques Poujol's excellent edition of the French of *La Monarchie.* And now Professor Kelley has once more examined the translation with the Vienna copy of the manuscript in hand.[52]

La Monarchie, one is told, is of interest to Romance philologists as an early example of "modern" French prose. This fact did not in any way affect my translation of *La Monarchie* or lead me to offer a more literal rendering. The fact that my English translation, though very close to the French, is no mere transliteration will in no way inconvenience philologists. Their concern will be with the French texts, not with their twentieth-century translation into English. The ordinary user of this volume—the non-French student of early modern political thought or politics who wants a quick insight into the way a shrewd early-sixteenth-century writer saw France and its politics—will probably prefer a lively, accurate translation to a boring, pre-

52. Discovered by Paula Sutter Fichtner and passed on through the good offices of Ruth Kleinman. With slight modifications the 1519 edition follows the Vienna MS. Verbal changes from the later editions (especially in parts 4 and 5) are minor and have not been indicated.

cise one. Therefore I have attempted a modified literal translation, modified in the sense that I have not permitted an
excessive appetite for literalness to interfere with my attempt
to prepare an English version that reads well and smoothly
and presents a minimum of ambiguities. Where the French
was most frequently ambiguous, that is, in the matter of reference, where it was not always clear to which of several possible antecedents a personal pronoun or possessive adjective
referred, I chose the antecedent that seemed to me most
likely and in translating restructured the sentence to remove
the ambiguity.

I have also restructured sentences that were quite unam-
biguous. In the various versions of *La Monarchie* the punctu-
ation is not uniform and the Seysselian sentences are often
exorbitantly long, not in response to the author's rhetorical
intent in such matters but rather to a certain insouciance and
absentmindedness on Seyssel's part or on the part of the
copyist or typesetter. In any event, I have not hesitated to
tighten sentence structure, to cut out some of the unnecessary connectives, and to make whatever changes that, not
affecting meaning, would render Seyssel's exposition a bit
more perspicuous, taut, and vigorous. It may have been this
policy that led Jacques Poujol to remark after reading the
translation in manuscript that it was more lively than the
original. To read that remark as praise for the translation is
imprudent; it is too ambivalent. Nevertheless it may be evidence that I managed to execute the policy of translation I
had adopted, whether or not the policy was a wise one.

"Policy" reminds me of one of the recurrent difficulties in
this translation, the key word "police." *Police* runs through
La Monarchie the way *virtù* runs through *Il Principe,* and it is
likewise a broad-spectrum word evocative of a considerable
range of meanings, a greater range in the sixteenth century
than now. An appendix has been provided to locate occur-
rences of the word "police" and derivations like "policié,"

and English renderings have been identified by an asterisk. Two other appendices present translations by Dr. Michael Sherman of Seyssel's prefaces to his translations of Justin and Appian. In general the text of the *Monarchy* and these prefaces follows the edition by Poujol, but afterthoughts, additions, and revisions have been added (from the Vienna manuscript, which is virtually the same as the printed edition of 1519) and placed within brackets. We hope that our efforts have given Seyssel an English dress as suitable as it is long-deserved.

DONALD R. KELLEY
University of Rochester
J. H. HEXTER
Washington University

The Monarchy of France

Proem of Messire Claude de Seyssel, Bishop of Marseille on the Monarchy of France, addressing the Most Christian King of France, Francis, First of that Name

Several philosophers, theologians and other wise men, most Christian and most happy king, have disputed, written, and dogmatized on what the government of the commonwealth in general ought to be, and among the several forms of government which is the best and most praiseworthy, and on these matters have been made many treatises and great volumes hard to read and to understand. It would be harder still, however, to put them into practice,[1] for in writing men set down what is desirable and what reason and natural sense quite readily teach; but human weakness is so great that no men are so wise, virtuous, and prudent as those the learned describe, nor similarly is there any city or republic, great or small, ruled entirely by moral and political reason, and few are without more imperfections than perfections. Therefore, to recite the arguments, reasons, and opinions of the authors treating these matters would be repetitious, prolix, and impossible or very difficult to follow, and would make a book the mere size of which would frighten off anyone who wanted to read it, unless he had a great deal of leisure. Even if he were willing to take the pains, after he had read it, he would remain confused and might blame the author for several parts of it. To gather in brief summary what may be useful in the management of the French monarchy; to

1. Cf. Aristotle *Politics* 4. 1. 1288^{b}34; 2. 12. 1273^{b}27; Machiavelli, *The Prince*, chap. 15.

consider how that monarchy was established and how it attained its present greatness; to deal with its faults, both those
of recent date and those recorded in the chronicles and histories of the deeds of the French, from which the monarchy
often suffered great harm, reverses, persecutions, and on
certain occasions almost complete ruin and destruction; in
addition to show how many good opportunities to perpetuate the realm the kings have lost; and to prepare a special
treatise about all these things would in my opinion be a
pleasant work worthy to present to a king newly come to the
throne and not possessed of that full understanding of this
monarchy which comes only with long practice. Now, my
lord, I have neither the knowledge nor the experience for
such a lofty task, especially since I am not a native of the
kingdom, and have not lived here nor dealt with such
matters long enough to understand the least part of the
realm's affairs, especially the important ones. The latter are
so broad and deep that men raised in the midst of them all
their lives can scarcely grasp them, however intelligent they
may be. Besides, in undertaking to write of such matters, I
could easily err in several points, and in any case subject myself to the judgment and the censure of all sorts of men who
are more ready to upbraid and condemn new things than to
do them; then, too, I might incur the ill will of those who
perhaps would find something adverse to their private designs. But if everyone stopped at such difficulties no one
would dare attempt it. So in order to incite the minds of men
better equipped to do the work and to give them material for
writing about it more fully, I, rather than to be silent as
others have been, have thought it better to make a start about
the little I saw and learned while living in the kingdom and
handling some of its principal affairs. For it would be more
pardonable to fail by too boldly undertaking a thing from
which understanding might profit and letters in no way suffer than out of fear to be marked as overbold to fail to set it
forth.

To this decision I am constrained by the affection and duty I owe to the French crown and nation, and, my lord, particularly and principally to you, both because you are now the moderator and monarch and because of my former obligation to you and your noble forebears both in the paternal and the maternal line.[2] I wish now to withdraw to the service of God and my church as my estate and age require; and I lack time and leisure to inform you by word of mouth of the many great matters I have dealt with. I am prevented from doing so by the grievous burdens with which you begin your reign as a result of the gathering of native and foreign princes and great persons, which was at your coronation greater than at those of any of your predecessors within memory. Still, in this short time it seems my duty at least to set down in writing not only the matters I have dealt with but also what I have learned from them. Then when the press of people and the business to be dispatched at the beginning of your reign abate and you have more leisure to consider the affairs of the kingdom, you will have no occasion to recall me from my church to render you an account of the charges I held, especially in the two last years of his reign, from the late king, your father-in-law, may he rest in peace.[3] For I leave you in writing far more than I would say by word of mouth, if I were present.

Although in my discourse I speak only in general terms, yet the observations are, I believe, reducible to particulars which require no great exposition. Besides, you have such

2. Seyssel served Charles VIII as well as Louis XII (father of Francis I's wife Claude) and the house of Savoy (from which came Francis's mother Louise).

3. From 1513, as bishop of Marseille, Seyssel was involved in negotiations with the papacy, arriving in Rome 24 July and attending the eighth (not ninth, as per Poujol) session of the Lateran Council, so opening the way to the Concordat of 1515. Louis XII died on 1 January 1515; Francis I was crowned 25 January; and Seyssel, having resigned his lay office (*maître des requêtes* in the Parlement of Paris), assumed his episcopal duties in April, after completing this book.

great and notable persons about you to conduct your principal affairs that they will understand more about them in a
moment than I could think, much less write, in a month.[4]
Where they are concerned, there is no need to make further
remarks; for several of them have seen much more of the past
affairs of your realm and other states and monarchies, and
have remembered them better than I. They have managed
the main affairs of the late king, your father-in-law, and of
two other kings, predecessors of yours, all three of whom
were wise and valiant princes who did noteworthy things.

The matters I had charge of all passed through the hands
of these persons, so that in the various letters I wrote while I
was in various places at the command and in the service of
the late king, they have seen everything I was able to learn
about those matters.[5] Nevertheless we are all mortal, and the
more things these men have seen and the more time they
have spent, the less time in the course of nature they have to
live. Because of their great tasks in conducting your affairs
they lack the leisure to set down in writing the things useful
for the future that they saw and learned in the past, and indeed, they need not do so since they are with you to give
their specific advice as situations come up, a far greater and
more important thing than to give it in theoretical discourse.
Therefore, being at leisure and having a lively memory of my
dealings and experience, I have sought to acquit myself by
communicating them not in the form of instruction, for it
would be very arrogant in a foreigner so unimportant and
ignorant as I to presume to give instructions on how he
should conduct himself to so wise a king surrounded by so
many notable persons, but in the form of a treatise, a thing

4. Especially the Chancelier Antoine du Prat; Jacques de Beaune
(Semblancay), *général des finances*; and the king's mother Louise and her
illegitimate brother René of Savoy.

5. Seyssel's extant correspondence has been published in the appendix
of Alberto Caviglia, *Claudio di Seyssel (1450–1520)* (Turin, 1928).

permissible to all men with some knowledge of letters and training in the moral sciences and history. For thus they only recount what they find written in authentic books. Although they lack practical experience of the affairs they write about and would be much more inexperienced at executing them than men trained in such matters who had read nothing about them, they have a greater opportunity to write of them following out what they find in the books they have read.[6]

Though in my treatise I have dealt in some detail with the affairs of France, even with respect to warfare and other matters not part of my profession, of which I could not have adequate experience, I have done so on the basis of information from many principal persons thoroughly trained in them and of knowledge so common as to be almost completely obvious to everyone. Besides, I have witnessed some things of these kinds and often been present when they were decided on by those in charge of them. Moreover, I have gone into details only in matters that I can demonstrate by political reason, approved authority, and authentic historical example, as did the Greek and Latin writers of treatises on polities* and republics, who were almost all scholarly men without experience of most of the things they wrote about. I have not had a chance to refresh my memory of these treatises while composing my little work because of the short time I could give to it—only the two months or thereabouts that I was among your followers between my return from Rome and my departure from the court. The greater part of this time I spent en route to your coronation and in some personal business.

Even if I had had time to examine those books, I would not have wanted to use them very extensively lest my work become too prolix and therefore disagreeable to you, my lord, and to others who might want to read it. For this reason

6. This commonplace that history is best written by men with firsthand experience was expressed most famously by Thucydides, whose own history had been translated into French by Seyssel just the year before (spring 1514).

I did not wish to follow the style or use the forms of those who have written of these matters before. Rather, in simple familiar style in ordinary everyday language, without alleging impressive reasons or authorities, I have touched on the points and events pertinent to my purpose, making no mention of any contemporary person, nor particularizing too much, seeking only as briefly as I can to give material to men with a far better understanding of these matters than I to write and speak of them more fully. To relieve such men somewhat of the trouble of keeping in mind the various parts of the work, and as an aid to understanding and memory, I have divided the book into five main parts. In the first I try to show how monarchical government and empire is the best of all polities, how that of France is the most civil and has the best polity* of all monarchies, past and present, and the reasons and means by which it attained to this greatness.[7] In the second I recall several political means* by which this monarchy of France can be preserved and increased. In the third the military force is dealt with, in the fourth relations with foreign princes and states, and in the fifth the way to undertake new wars and conquests and keep and preserve newly conquered lands.

All of the four last parts tend to one end, to show how and by what means the French monarchy can be preserved and increased. For the greater convenience of the readers, because this section would be very elaborate compared with the first, I have divided it in four, and for the same reason I have divided each part into separate chapters more or less long depending on the subject matter.

I beg you most humbly, my lord, to be pleased to accept and find agreeable this little gift I make to you on the occa-

7. Seyssel's "grandeur" is an example of his Italianate political vocabulary (see also pt. 1, nn. 23, 27), parallel to "grandezza," appearing, for example, in Dino Campagni's fourteenth-century *Cronica*, 1:1, and other works up to the time of Machiavelli.

sion of your joyous accession to the crown and to take it in good part since it proceeds from good intention. If you find anything in it that applies to the conduct of your affairs, take what seems good, and supply the rest by your sound sense and prudence and by the counsel of men of the better sort whom you have chosen to manage your principal affairs, as you have started to do very well indeed. By so doing and by using the sharpness of mind and liveliness of heart that God endowed you with as well as the personal inclinations natural to your age, with God's help and the opportunities that time and events will bring you, you can render this your realm the happiest and most renowned that ever has been. And to the great number of men now in France and elsewhere who delight in writing of such matters in Latin and French and who know how to do so, you can give material by which they can leave a perpetual memorial of your virtuous deeds greater than any of your predecessors for a long time.

And giving all the glory and honor to God and living in fear of Him, as you were wont to do in all things up to now, you will be ranged in the rank and number of good, virtuous, and catholic princes, in this world through a glorious and perpetual fame, in the other through an eternal reward, by means of the infinite mercy and goodness of Him from whom proceed all good things, all honor, and all happiness earthly and heavenly.

Here Begins the Monarchy of France

CHAPTER I

The Monarchic State in General, and That
It Is Better Than Any Other

FIRST PART

Without going too deeply into the disputes of the philosophers, we may presuppose three kinds of political rule:
monarchy under a single person, aristocracy under a certain
number of the better sort, and democracy the popular state
[*regime et gouvernement populaire*].[1] Of these, according to the
true and most widespread opinion, monarchy is the best if
the prince is good and has the sense, the experience, and the
good will to govern justly. That rarely comes to pass, however, because with such authority and license it is hard to
follow the right course and hold fairly the balance of justice.
The second state seems the more reasonable and praiseworthy since it is more lasting, better founded, and easier to bear
[, being comprised of the persons selected by the assembly or
a part of them. Such persons are, moreover, subject to corruption and change, at least to the extent that, when there are
several bad and inadequate men among them, the better
sort, being their superiors, can repress their boldness and
thwart their unreasonable enterprises.] As to the popular

1. Aristotle *Politics* 3. 7. 1279ª22; Plato *Republic* 8. 544. Poujol has title of
chap. 1, as below chap. 6, second part, chaps. 1, 2, 3 'section' headings, but
this sectioning is not followed in Vienna MS and printed editions.

state, it has always been turbulent, dangerous, and hostile to the better sort. Nevertheless, the aristocratic state is often transformed into oligarchy, a monopoly by covetous and ambitious folk, who, though chosen as the wisest and most prudent of the people to rule and to govern the people well, care only for their particular profit. So when all is said, none of these states can possibly be perpetual, for ordinarily in the course of time they get worse, especially when they go on growing, so that often one [by disorder] rises from the other.

CHAPTER II
Of the State and Empire of the Romans, and Its
[Perfections and] Imperfections

This we can apprehend clearly from the state of the Roman Empire which [in the judgment of all wise men and according to their writings and experience] was the greatest of all and had the best polity* of all, yet it passed from the monarchy of the kings to the rule of the Decemvirs, then to popular rule, then again to monarchy.[2] Especially was it long ruled and governed by the consuls and the senate under the authority of the people. During this government it fared best and went on continually expanding until it went back to monarchy. In truth this state was so arranged that it shared traits of all three forms.[3] The consuls had sovereign authority during their consulate over several matters even when out of the city; and nevertheless the senate, made up of personages esteemed the wisest and most prudent of the people, held the

2. Polybius *History* 6. 4; cf. Augustine *City of God* 2. 21 and 19. 21. The Roman pattern was reflected not only in Livy but also in various authors translated by Seyssel, especially Justin, Diodorus Siculus, and Appian, and in civil law, especially Digest 1, 2, 2, "On the Origin of Law," on which Seyssel commented; contemporaneously it was also combined with the Polybian *anacyclosis* by Aymar du Rivail, *Historia juris civilis* (Paris, 1515).

3. Polybius *History* 6. 11.

rudder of the ship in the principal matters, so that scarcely anything of prime importance could be done without its authority. The people too had a major role in the government, in selecting officers, in deciding on peace and war, and in several other acts [and matters of great importance]. And besides they had their tribunes, without whom the senate could not make a valid decree.

For these reasons this was the best form of government of a community and popular empire at that time or since. Experience proves this, because under this government the Romans ruled the greater part of the world. Nevertheless, in reading of their deeds and histories we find much imperfection, as can be judged both from moral reason and experience. Without seeking to enumerate all the points where we can observe this imperfection I will mention several of the chief and most obvious which caused the ruin of the popular empire and its return to a monarchy, which since has come to nothing or to a trifling matter, as can be seen.

In brief, from the beginning, when they established a popular state and government after the kings were driven away, the senate and nobles took so much authority and left so little to the lesser folk that the latter mutinied and seceded from them with great dissension. To appease these people they had to give them more authority than was reasonable. Later, from this cause rose all the civil divisions which, except for truces in times of great external crisis, were continual. This was not the case under the kings, for the people will much more easily bear subjection and obedience to a sole prince than to a crowd of folk to whom they often deem themselves equal. If the people are granted any authority, in the long run they will want most of it, whereupon disorder will follow as it did to the popular state of the Romans. For the authority of the people became too great both in the power of the tribunes, who prevented many good things and did many ill, and in the selection of officers and leaders in war and in the work of police,* which most often, especially[4] in times of peace and prosperity, was made on the basis of ambition and corruption. In this way those who by gifts, by promises, or by other illicit means could win the favor of the people were preferred to good and notable persons zealous for the common weal. Whence it came about that to reimburse themselves for the outlays they made in gaining office and providing largesse for the people, the men elected and deputed to office by such means engaged in great pillage, extortion, and violence against both the subjects and the friends and allies of the Roman Empire.

Moreover, they permitted the warriors and mercenaries to imitate them in everything they did, both in order to win the favor and good will of the soldiers and because, had they wished to punish them, the troops would not have borne it readily but would have said in reproach that they took example from their rulers. Thus, military discipline was totally destroyed. Thus too was vitiated the true and ancient polity,* introduced at the outset by the old prudent founders of the empire and long maintained until wealth and grandeur smothered it and engendered dissolution and corruption.

Thence did the civil wars have their beginning among the Romans; for men unable to get the management of great affairs and honorable offices in the city by merit, beneficence, and authority of the senate found chances to win the favor of the people by persuading them to self-indulgent courses on the pretext of the common weal. These men did this in order to get the people into disputes with the senate and the better sort, hoping by these means and by popular favor to gain the chief authority in the city and oppress the senate and leading citizens. This was what the two Gracchi, the initiators of the agrarian law, did. And out of this discord and dispute, soon after, came the other great civil strife between Marius and

4. Vienna MS reads *mesmement* instead of *principalement*.

Sulla, the more pernicious in that, besides corrupting all military discipline, it deprived the senate and the officials of the obedience of the commanders and soldiers, so that the man in control of [arms and] troops did what he pleased, and thus had the upper hand in the field and town, and ceased to obey the senate at all. He usurped all authority, disposed all things according to his will, and regardless of their condition of life, dignity, and authority, even persecuted with slaughter and every cruelty those who had held to the opposing party. Sulla and Marius did this first, and following their example Julius Caesar, and afterwards in consequence [the triumvirate of Marcus Antonius, Lepidus, and Octavius, and then Octavius against the other two until he held the monarchy alone; and even later he did many evil things, as did almost all emperors after him].

This can be seen and recognized in the faults of popular government, which many wise and prudent men, zealous for the public weal, perceived before the drawbacks became manifest. They warned of them but could not cure them. We must conclude therefore that if the chief authority rests with the people, the popular regime cannot be perfect even though it has the traits of the other two.[5]

CHAPTER III
Of the State and Empire of the Venetians, and Its Perfections
[and Imperfections]

The aristocratic form is much better, since in the hands of a certain number of the leading citizens who govern it by good laws it can maintain itself, as in my opinion Venice does. It has some trace of monarchy in the doge. There is nothing popular about it, as the people have no governmental authority but are entirely subject to the signory, which, how-

5. In Vienna MS and printed editions this sentence begins chap. 3.

ever, maintains them in their liberties and rights, so that they have no cause to rebel. They are also restrained and humbled by rigorous laws. By these means has the signory achieved its present grandeur, and maintained and preserved it against several powerful princes, so that it has held up in the end although it has suffered much. In truth it is the most perfect and best policed* empire and republican state which we have seen or read about up to now. Those who know about the Venetian laws, customs, and manner of life, agree on this score.[6] Still, there are imperfections which have often caused it to be placed in great travail and several times in danger of complete ruin, and which may do so again in the future. From whatever cause, it must come to pass that this regime and all others that are or will be in the world come to an end. For there is nothing eternal under heaven, and all that begins must end, even these mystical bodies, which are like material human bodies, created and composed of four contrary elements and humors.[7] For a while they may be maintained and kept alive so long as the humors are in harmony; but in the long run one humor must transcend the others and by dissolution of the bond the mass will entirely return to its original condition. By the order of nature, once they are assembled all those elements and humors go

6. For Venice, Seyssel could draw not only on such authors as Sabellico and Giustiniani but also on his own experiences, already expressed in his *La Victoire du Roi contre les Venitiens* (Paris, 1510). Cf. Machiavelli, *Discourses* 1. 5, 6, 50. The "myth of Venice," enhanced by its victory in 1509 during the war of the League of Cambrai, has been discussed in the Florentine and English context but not much in relation to France, aside from Béatrix Rava, *Venise dans la littérature française* (Paris, 1916), esp. pp. 234–36, and Michael Sherman, "Political Propaganda and Renaissance Culture: French Reactions to the League of Cambrai, 1509–1510," *Sixteenth Century Journal* 8 (1977): 97–128. For a comparison of Machiavelli and Seyssel see Innocenzo Cervelli, *Machiavelli e la crisi della stato veneziano* (Naples, 1974), chap. 7.

7. See Ralph E. Giesey, "The French Estates and the Corpus Mysticum Regni," in *Album Helen Maud Cam* (Louvain, 1960), pp. 155–71, and Ernst H. Kantorowicz, *The King's Two Bodies* (Princeton, 1957), chap. 5.

through increase, stability, and decline. When this happens, we must aid nature and support the most feeble member and humor, yet when we do try to aid one we injure another. This also happens in the mystical bodies of human society, for after they are assembled in one civil and political union they go on for a while increasing and multiplying; after that they remain stable a while longer; then, since they are composed of several discordant and conflicting understandings and wills, they begin to decline and finally are annihilated.

There are in fact five ages of the mystical as of the human body—infancy the beginning, youth the growth, manhood the apogee, old age the decline, and decrepitude the dissolution.[8] According to these ages and degrees the Roman Empire has been described and divided by several notable authors and historians. Returning to our subject of the aristocratic state and government of the Venetians, there exist in it several discordant elements which so far have been the occasion of many troubles and will be hard to handle in the long run. Thus the gentlemen who are lords have complete dominion and divide among themselves all or most of those offices and charges from which honors and profit flow. Therefore the other citizens, many of whom are wise, rich, and spirited men, are tremendously envious and discontented, especially because the number of the gentlemen and lords has so increased in the course of time as to be excessive now. On the other hand, in cities and territories subject to them the nobles and powerful men are kept very low because this signory has always feared that, having credit and authority with the people, they might stir them to mutiny. So the leading citizens have no hope of gaining any important office, of which there are not half enough for the lords.

Another evil, and no small one, is that for fear that one of them might usurp the government if he had authority over

8. Lucius Anneus Florus, *The Two Books of the Epitome*, trans. E. Forster (New York, 1929), bk. 1; cf. Lactantius *The Divine Institutes* 7. 15.

both the people and the military in his hands, they scarcely ever give natives overall or subordinate commands, especially not over the land forces, but usually put their army in the charge of foreigners. In truth, since they are more inclined to trade than to war, few of them are [very often] good commanders or even good soldiers. As foreigners, their commanders and most of their troops have not the zeal and affection for the signory and republic that those to whom it belongs would have. Although they give the captain-generals and military leaders attendants and adjutants called supervisors,[9] without whom the commanders cannot do or order anything important even in military matters, this is not an adequate remedy, for the supervisors are not military men and may easily make serious blunders. The commanders, finding themselves subordinate to and constrained to obey them in professional matters which they do not understand, often become disdainful and do not serve wholeheartedly, as they would if they had full authority, but sometimes are quite well pleased when things done against their will to suit the whim of the supervisors miscarry, as has often happened.

There is, moreover, factional dispute among the gentlemen and lords, between those descended from the ancient founders of the city and those created subsequently, who are now more numerous than the ancient families. Each faction tries to have the main authority both in the management of the republic and in offices and other honors and profits. Whence it often happens that in the business of the state they are in disagreement and split into parties having more regard to their particular desires than to the public weal, to which desires they are as subject as other folk. Because of the good sense and skill of the wiser men no great evil has yet resulted from this, but in the long run there is a great danger that when the evil humors of the mystical body

9. On the "provideteurs" (*provedditori*) see also Philippe de Commynes, *Mémoires*, bk. 7, pt. 18 and bk. 8, pt. 9.

become too numerous and poisonous, they will discover the sickness too severe to remedy in time.

CHAPTER IV

The Conclusion That Results from the Premises That the Monarchic State Is Best

I say these things here not because it is within my province or intention to condemn the state and government of the Venetians. I affirm that it is to my mind the best ordered* and established of any of the aristocratic states I have seen or read about; but I want to show that there are bound to be more imperfections in such a regime, even when great and powerful, than in a monarchical regime. For a single head and monarch can better remedy and obviate all dangers and difficulties than can an assembly of folk elected to govern but nonetheless subject to those whom they govern. He is always better obeyed, revered, feared, and esteemed, whether the community be great or small, than a temporary and removable head or one without full authority. Divine and human, natural and political reason all prove that it is always necessary to revert to a single head in all things and that a plurality of heads is pernicious.[10] Experience also shows that several monarchical states, as for example, those of the Egyptians, the Assyrians and the Parthians, have lasted longer than any aristocratic, democratic, or popular ones. And they have been more peaceful and have had fewer changes and civil dissensions, although the heads and monarchs often changed by death or otherwise. And the same is true of the monarchies of our own time, the kingdom of England, of Spain, and especially of France, for these have already lasted longer as monarchical orders than any great popular or aristocratic state that we know of.

10. Cf. Thomas Aquinas, *De Regimine Principum*, chap. 2.

CHAPTER V
How It Is Better That Princes and Monarchs Rule by Succession
Than by Election

It can be seen by experience that regimes in which authority
passes by succession prosper more than those in which it
passes by election, as it appears from the Roman Empire in
comparison with others.[11] The reason for this is clear, since
to attain to conditions of life so great and so honorable men
will resort to any practice or intrigue; and usually it ends in
violence, as has happened several times in the elections of
emperors and sultans.[12] Please God, it has not happened and
never will hereafter to the papacy and other ecclesiastical
dignities where complete purity, charity, and honesty
should rule. As I insisted at the beginning, from these reasons and examples and others that I might mention but leave
aside to avoid prolixity, one can conclude that the government and state of France is much better established under a
monarch than if it were an aristocracy or democracy, that is
to say, in the hands of some small number of chosen folk or
of the whole people.

CHAPTER VI
That the French Monarchy in Particular Is Better Regulated
Than Any Other

Unless it had other special traits, however, the monarchy of
France would be no different in this respect from that of
other monarchical states governed after the same fashion.
Nevertheless, I wish to show that the monarchy of France is

11. The superiority of (the French) hereditary monarchy to (the German)
elective empire, based on canonist authority, was commonly argued by
contemporary jurists, including Jean Ferrault, Barthélemy de Chasseneux (a
former student of Seyssel), Charles de Grassaile, and Charles Dumoulin.

12. The Ottoman Empire had recently (1511–13) experienced a war of succession between the sons of Sultan Bayazid.

governed by a much better order than any others now existing or known from ancient history, because it not only has
lasted long, and preserved and maintained itself, but has
prospered, come to greater power and dominion, and corrected some of its own imperfections, of which I will speak
hereafter. This correction is easy when the prince is willing
to make it.

CHAPTER VII

How It Is Well That the Realm Passes by Masculine Succession

The first special trait that I find good is that this realm passes
by masculine succession and, by virtue of the law which the
French call Salic, cannot fall into the hands of a woman.[13]
This is excellent, for by falling into the feminine line it can
come into the power of a foreigner, a pernicious and dangerous thing, since a ruler from a foreign nation is of a different
rearing and condition, of different customs, different language, and a different way of life from the men of the lands
he comes to rule. He ordinarily, therefore, wishes to advance
those of his nation, to grant them the most important authority in the handling of affairs, and to prefer them to honors and profits. Moreover, he always has more love for and
faith in them and so conforms more to their customs and
ways than to the customs of the land to which he has newly
come, whence there always follows envy and dissension

13. *La Loy Salique, premiere loy des François* (1464), whoever wrote it, first
published in Rouen in 1488, appeared in the 1541 edition of the *Monarchy*
and was thereafter misattributed to Seyssel. In general see J. M. Potter, "The
Development and Significance of the Salic Law of the French," *English Historical Review* 52 (1937): 235–53, and Ralph E. Giesey, *The Juristic Basis of
Dynastic Right to the French Throne, Transactions of the American Philosophical
Society*, vol. 51, pt. 5 (Philadelphia, 1961). In violation of this law Henry VIII
had recently declared himself "King of France" and Louis XII only "King of
the French."

between the natives and the foreigners and indignation against the princes, as has often been seen by experience, and is seen all the time. When the succession goes from male to male, the heir is always certain and is of the same blood as those who formerly ruled, so the subjects have the very same love and reverence for him as for his predecessors. Even though he be related only distantly and the dead king have daughters, yet without deviation or scruple the people turn to him as soon as the other has ceased to be, and there is no disturbance or difficulty. So it went at the death of King Charles VIII and of King Louis XII recently deceased. Although in former times there were great quarrels and differences on such occasions, which brought great wars, persecutions, and desolations to the realm, nevertheless, these differences were not the reason for the troubles but the pretext, although well known to be frivolous and ill founded. In the end matters must have been redressed and so established that there can never again be dissensions and difficulties on this score. [In order to demonstrate what I have said about the perfection of the monarchy of France I have included in this account] the state of France as it is now, joining the old laws, customs, and observances with the new and more recent.

CHAPTER VIII
How the Authority and Power of the King Is Regulated and Bridled in France by Three Bridles

Another thing, which I esteem the main one for the conservation and augmentation of this monarchy, is that its head and all its members are regulated with such good order that they scarcely can fall into great [dissension and] disharmony by any means, at least until by the will of God and by the common course of nature, which cannot create or produce

anything perpetual and immune from corruption and mutation, the time of decline and dissolution comes. This must
happen sooner or later, as we have said above at the very
outset. Yet, as mortal men live longer and in better health
insofar as they are of better constitution and live under a
better regimen, so the lordships and states which are best
established and ordered* maintain themselves longer and in
better condition. To express more clearly my meaning concerning the polity* of France, I assume that the greatest
danger to monarchical states comes from the turmoil and
confusion caused by change of princes even when they succeed by natural succession of the nearest male heir, as they
do here. It often happens that to a good and brave king there
succeeds a feeble one, or one blemished by [vices and] imperfections, or indeed a baby. Disorderly and willful action
follows because of the bad government of such a vicious
monarch or of those who have the guidance of an infant or
idiot king. This may occasion great destruction and desola-
tion of the whole state, as can be seen by several examples in
this very realm. Without fail, when by the ordinance of God
vengeance smites the realm, such destruction will occur in
this way or one like it, preordained by divine wisdom and
providence which human reason and prudence cannot resist.[14] This may happen at the moment when there is the
greatest appearance of prosperity and the least of change and
adversity, in order that men, deceived by mundane things,
may better know their fragility and instability and the power
and providence of God, as we can see clearly enough in our
time and read in many old histories. [May God never let this
happen here, at least so long as there remains a king of this
noble and ancient race.]

But coming back to my theme and speaking according to

14. The canonist theme, "translation of empire," was based on *Ecclesias-
ticus* (Catholic Bible) 10. 8: "God transfers kingdom from one people to
another because of injustice, injuries, blasphemies, and other evils"; cf.
Werner Goez, *Translatio Imperii* (Tübingen, 1958).

human reason, I say that the remedies planned to avoid such evils when they come are far more prompt and certain in this monarchy than in any other. Thus, with respect to the disorders which may result from the imperfections of monarchs, there are several remedies to check their absolute authority if they are unrestrained and willful, and more still to check those who have the custody of the realm if the monarch is entirely incapacitated by youth or otherwise. Yet the royal dignity and authority remains always entire, not totally absolute[15] nor yet too much restrained, but regulated and bridled by good laws, ordinances, and customs established in such a way that they can scarcely be broken or reduced to nothing, even though in some times and places some violence is done in them. Of these bridles by which the absolute power of the king of France is regulated I deem that there are three main ones. The first is religion, the second justice, the third the polity.*

CHAPTER IX

Of Religion, Which Is the First Bridle of the King

As to the first, it is certain that the people of France have always been and still are devout and religious above all other people and nations. For even when they were given over to superstition and idolatry, as was almost all the rest of the world, they were very observant therein, so that the Druids, the preservers of this superstition, had total authority over them, as Caesar tells in his *Commentaries*.[16] When the Christian faith appeared, France was among the first of the distant

---

15. At issue here is the civilian formula *princeps legibus solutus est*, on which see B. Tierney, "The Prince is not Bound by the Laws," *Comparative Studies in Society and History* 5 (1963): 388ff, and A. Bossuat, "The Maxim 'The King is Emperor in his Kingdom': Its Use in the Fifteenth Century before the Parlement," in *The Recovery of France in the Fifteenth Century*, ed. Peter S. Lewis (New York, 1971), pp. 185–95.

16. Caesar *The Gallic Wars* 6. 13–14.

nations to receive it, and having received it kept it completely and constantly beyond all other realms and peoples without ever nourishing any monster of heresy, as St. Jerome bears witness. The English, the Germans, the Spaniards, and other neighboring nations often and at divers times have received or reformed their faith after that of the Gauls and the French, and the princes and peoples of France always have been more ardent and more prompt than any others to wipe out heretics and infidels and to defend the Roman Catholic church. Even to this day all the nations of Christianity come to learn theology at the University of Paris, as the true fountain whence flows forth the perfect doctrine. Therefore, this realm is called most Christian and the kings most Christian.[17]

So it is essential that whoever is king here make known to the people by example and by present and overt demonstration that he is a zealous observant of the Christian faith and wishes to maintain and augment it to the best of his ability. If the people had another opinion of him, they would hate him and perhaps obey him but ill. Moreover, this people would impute all the troubles that came to the realm to the erroneous creed and imperfect religion of the king. Thence might result many great scandals, as has happened several times formerly, although the disorders came rather through the fault of other folk than of the kings. Of this I do not want to speak further for it is common knowledge.[18]

If the king lives in accordance with the Christian religion and law [at least in appearance] he can scarcely act tyrannically, and if he does so act, it is permissible for any prelate or any other man of religion who leads a good life and holds the

17. *Rex Christianissimus* was another formula much discussed by contemporary jurists; in general see Jean de Pange, *Le Roi très chrétien* (Paris, 1949).

18. A review of these was presented in 1511 by Jean Lemaire de Belges in *Le Traicté Intitulé de la difference des schismes et des conciles de leglise*, in J. Lemaire de Belges, *Oeuvres*, ed. J. Stecher (Louvain, 1885), 3:231–359.

people in esteem to remonstrate with him and censure him
and for a simple preacher to reprehend him publicly to his
face.[19] Truly, although the king might want to, he would not
dare mistreat or harm the men who do this, for fear of
provoking the ill will and indignation of the people. This is
not the way it is in other realms, at least as far as one knows.
Moreover, the kings are so instructed and habituated in religion from their childhood with a traditional reverence that
they can scarcely go so far astray that they cease to fear God
and to reverence prelates and churchmen of good renown.
This color and appearance of religion and of having God on
their side has always brought great favor, obedience, and
reverence to princes, as can be seen in old histories. Without being prolix about examples, this is obvious from what
Alexander the Great did, who said he was engendered by the
god Jupiter; and all the ancient kings and great captains of
Greece said they were descended directly from the gods. Because he feigned to do all things by the advice of the gods
and to have consultations[20] with the goddess Egeria, Numa
Pompilius reduced the Roman people to a more profound
obedience than Romulus had done by high and chivalric
deeds and by military discipline. It is said likewise of
Scipio Africanus that he feigned to speak to the gods and
to undertake enterprises by their advice. To speak of Christian princes, Constantine the Great, Theodosius, Charlemagne, and several others have greatly prospered by being
zealous for the Christian religion and by the general belief
that they were so.

Understanding that they must live [in esteem and repu-
tation] as good Christians in order to have the love and com-

19. Seyssel's emphasis on the "appearance" of piety, recalling the famous
advice of Machiavelli (*The Prince*, chap. 18), represents corrections in Vienna
MS.

20. Seyssel's word is "conference": according to Plutarch, Numa married
Egeria; cf. Livy 1. 21. 3, etc., and Arrian *Anabasis of Alexander* 4. 9; 5. 10; 7. 8.

plete obedience of the people, even though they themselves
were not sufficiently dedicated to devotion to God and fear of
Him, the kings of France have avoided doing outrageous and
reprehensible things, if not always and in everything at least
ordinarily. This is, as we have said, the first rein and bridle
of the kings of France.

CHAPTER X
Of Justice, Which Is the Second Bridle

The second bridle is justice, which beyond any doubt is in
greater authority in France than in any other country of the
world that we know of, especially on account of the Parlements, which were instituted chiefly to bridle the absolute
power that the kings might want to use. From the very outset
they were staffed with such great persons in such number
and of such power that the kings have always been subject to
them with respect to distributive justice.[21] So one can have
justice and right against kings as well as against subjects in
civil matters; and in cases between private parties the royal
authority cannot prejudice the right of others, but on the
contrary the king's letters and rescripts are subject to the

21. Cf. Aristotle *Politics* 3. 9. 1280²8; 4. 16. 1300ᵇ13; and Machiavelli, *Discourses* 3. 1 (trans. A. Gilbert, *Machiavelli: The Chief Works* [Durham, 1965],
1:422): "Kingdoms also need to be renewed and to have their laws brought
back toward their beginnings. We see what good results this plan produces
in the kingdom of France, which lives under laws and under regulations
more than any other kingdom." On the function of the parlements see Jean
Montaigne, *Tractatus celebris de auctoritate et preeminentia sacri Magni consilii
et Parlamentorum* (Paris, 1509). On royal institutions in and before Seyssel's
time see especially the identically titled and dated works of Roger Doucet
and Gaston Zeller, *Les Institutions de la France au XVIe siècle* (Paris, 1948);
John S. C. Bridge, *France in 1515*, vol. 5, *A History of France from the death of
Louis XI* (Oxford, 1936); and Peter S. Lewis, *Later Medieval France* (London,
1968).

judgments of the Parlements, not touching obreption and subreption only, as it is with other princes according to the Roman law, but also with respect to legality and illegality.[22]

Royal graces and remissions in criminal cases are so thoroughly debated in Parlement and those who obtain them put through such interrogation that few people dare do any misdeed, through hope or confidence in them. Although occasionally, on account of the too-great favor of a willful king, men dare not take legal action in such a case, yet in the long run the king repents; and so finally, when this inordinate favor has ceased, they who had it, or their heirs, are more sharply punished than if they had not made use of it. So it has been and will always be in the future. This justice is the more authoritative because the officers deputed to administer it are permanent; and it is not in the power of the king to depose them except for malfeasance, of which the cognizance is reserved to the sovereign courts in the first instance with respect to their own members, and on appeal with respect to inferior courts. If, by an act of unregulated will, judges on occasion have been deprived regardless of order, those who were responsible or those who took over their office have later been brought to account for it and removed. So it comes about that those judges and officers, knowing themselves irremovable if they do no wrong, acquit themselves in the administration of justice with greater confidence, or, if they do not, are inexcusable. Truly, as has been said, this rein and bridle is greater and more praiseworthy in France than in any other land, and has been maintained for so long that it

22. The reformation of justice is the subject of the *ordonnances* of March 1498 and June 1510, printed in *Recueil général des anciennes lois françaises*, ed. François Isambert et al. (Paris, 1821–33), vol. 11, nos. 26 and 98 (hereafter cited as Isambert); and cf. Edouard Maugis, *Histoire du Parlement de Paris* (Paris, 1913), 1:539ff. *Obreptio* implies the concealing of facts, *surreptio* outright lying, to gain an advantage (see Adolf Berger, *Encyclopedic Dictionary of Roman law* [Philadelphia, 1953]).

scarcely can be broken, although it may be bent, and although there are imperfections in this justice as in all other human affairs.

CHAPTER XI
Of the Polity, Which Is the Third Bridle

The third bridle is that of polity,*[23] that is to say, the many ordinances, made by the kings of France themselves and afterwards confirmed and approved from time to time, which tend to the conservation of the realm in general and in detail. These have been kept for such a long time that the princes never undertake to derogate from them; and if they wanted to do so, their commands would not be obeyed, especially as to their domain and royal patrimony, which they cannot alienate except in case of necessity.[24] Such alienation must come under the cognizance of and be approved by the sovereign courts of parlement and by the chambers of accounts—which in these matters proceed so deliberately and with such delay and discussion that, knowing such alienations to be neither valid nor secure and realizing that they may be required to return what they take by virtue of them, few people purchase them. Moreover, although the kings can

23. For a discussion of "police" and "polizza" see Henri Estienne, *Deux Dialogues du nouveau langage François italianizé*, ed. I[sidore] L[iseux] (Paris, 1883), 1:96–97. "Police" or "policié" was used earlier by Nicolas Oresme, Commynes, and Lemaire de Belges (see Frédéric Godefoy, *Dictionnaire de l'ancienne langue française*, 10 vols. [Paris, 1881–1902] and Edmond Huguet, *Dictionnaire de la langue française du XVIe siècle*, 7 vols. [Paris, 1925]) and especially in the ordinances (Isambert). For Seyssel's usage see appendix 3.

24. Cf. François Olivier-Martin, *Histoire du droit français* (Paris, 1951), pp. 319ff; André Lemaire, *Les Lois fondamentales de la monarchie française d'après les théoriciens de l'ancien régime* (Paris, 1907); and in general Peter Riesenberg, *Inalienability of Sovereignty in Medieval Political Thought* (New York, 1956).

dispose according to their whim of the yield and revenue of the realm during the time that they are its administrators, all expenditures ordinary and extraordinary must go back to the chamber of accounts, which often retrenches and limits those that are ill grounded.[25] This law is very useful to the commonwealth for the conservation of the royal domain, whose depletion forces the king in case of a crisis to fall back on extraordinary exactions which burden and aggrieve the people. In this way, too, the overgreat liberality of princes, tending toward prodigality, is restrained.

CHAPTER XII
*How This Moderation and Bridling of the Absolute Power
of Kings Is to Their Own Great Honor and Profit*

To avoid prolixity I do not wish to speak of the many other laws and ordinances observed concerning the public weal of the realm. It suffices me to have explained the above three bridles and restraints on the absolute power of the kings, which because of them is not of less but rather of greater dignity, because better regulated. If it were more ample and absolute, it would be worse and more imperfect, just as the power of God is not judged less but rather more perfect because He cannot sin or do ill. Because with all their great authority and power they are willing to be subject to their own laws and live according to them, kings are more laudable than if they could at their whim make use of absolute power.[26] Thus, as a result of their goodness and tolerance their monarchic authority, regulated by the means already

25. On the *Chambre des comptes* see the *ordonnance* of 20 March 1500 (Isambert, vol. 11, no. 46).
26. Cf. Aristotle *Politics* 3. 14. 1284^{b}35 and 5. 10. 1310^{a}39, and John Fortescue, *De Laudibus Legum Anglie*, ed. S. Chrimes (Cambridge, 1942).

spoken of, has some of the traits of the aristocracy, which renders it more complete and perfect and also more firm and lasting.

CHAPTER XIII
Of the Three Estates of the People of France and How They Are Well Regulated and Supported

Besides this, and tending to the same effect, there is another praiseworthy ordering and way of life in this realm, carefully to be preserved for the union and accord of all the estates. They have been so well set afoot and continued that the realm can scarcely fall into great decadence while they are well maintained, since each estate has its own rights and preeminences according to its quality, and one estate can scarcely oppress the other, nor all three together conspire against the head and monarch. Among these three estates I do not include that of the church, concerning which I will speak later; but I take them to be as they are in other realms, that is to say, the nobility, the middle people which might be called the rich people, and the lesser folk.[27]

CHAPTER XIV
Of the Estate of the Nobility [and Its Maintenance]

The first estate, the nobility, is better dealt with than in any other land that we know of, for it has at the outset several great prerogatives and preeminences over the other two. By means of these it is always bound to the prince, well affected toward him, and ready to serve him in all matters and to risk goods and life for the defense of the realm and the service of

27. The distinction of *popolo grasso-popolo minuto* dates at least from Dante's time: see Dino Compagni, *Cronica*, 1:17.

the king.[28] It is in the first place free of all *gabelles, tailles,* and levies laid on the other two estates, a great privilege, and carefully preserved. Secondly, because to the nobility belongs the defense of the king and the realm, all gentlemen may lawfully bear arms everywhere, even in the king's chamber, a thing usually prohibited to the others. Thirdly, if they do not wish to remain in their own households, there are divers means to maintain them in the noble way of life, refraining from mechanical or mercenary trades which are forbidden to them. A great many serve the king in the various offices of his household, not all at once but one quarter at a time; for it would be tumultuous otherwise on account of the multitude of offices. This also gives each one time to take care of his own household affairs. Serving in their turn, they all have ordinary wages on which they can maintain themselves and always hope for better.

The princes of the blood and other great lords all have some position or income from the king and maintain thereby a great number of other men according to their rank. And similarly the counts, barons, and other powerful and rich gentlemen maintain fewer, each according to his ability. Although this is also done in other lands, it is not done so amply and on such a scale. Moreover, the regular cavalry is larger and better paid and maintained here than anywhere else. It was instituted for the defense of the realm and to have always a sufficient number of mounted men trained in arms and also for the maintenance of gentlemen. These charges are so divided that many nobles of diverse condition can be maintained honorably although the realm is not at war. For according to their own quality and valor the magnates have charge of more or fewer horsemen. Other gentlemen are lieutenants, others ensign-bearers, others men-at-arms,

28. Cf. Doucet, *Les Institutions de la France*, 2:488ff, and Etienne Dravasa, *"Vivre noblement," Recherches sur la dérogeance de noblesse du XIVe au XVIe siècles* (Bordeaux, 1965).

others archers [and yet others young gentlemen pages. These *gens d'ordonnance*] are relieved of duties when not needed so that they can live part of the time in their own houses and save a part of their wages.[29]

There are, moreover, an unbelievable number of offices and charges in this realm to distribute among the nobility. Such are the *gouverneurs* of lands and provinces, the *baillages, sénéschausées, châtellanies,* captaincies of towns, and several others, not to mention the chief offices belonging to great persons appointed for life—the constable, the marshalls, the grand master, the admiral, and other such.[30] The king gives pensions in his establishment and according to his will to several who have no office or charge and are not ordinary officers of his household.

Indeed, this estate should be content, for it seems to be better sustained than either of the other two. Reason, of course, requires this both because the members of this estate are bound to the defense of the realm, and because of their own merits and services, but also because of those of their ancestors. The other two estates, however, are neither forgotten nor ill treated.

CHAPTER XV
Of the Middling Estate, or the Rich People, and Its Maintenance

As to the second, the middling people, it is very well maintained and has good reason to be satisfied, for to it pertains commerce.[31] The commercial activity is well supported with-

29. On the *compagnies d'ordonnance* see Doucet, *Les Institutions de la France,* 2:620ff.

30. *Ordonnances* on *connêtable* and *maréchal* (undated, reign of Louis XII) and *amiral,* July 1517 (Isambert, vol. 11, no. 128 and vol. 12, no. 54); and cf. Doucet, *Les Institutions de la France,* 1:229ff.

31. *Ordonnance* of April 1515 on privileges of Parisian bourgeoisie (Isambert, vol. 12, no. 27). Cf. Aristotle *Politics* 4. 11. 1295^{b}2. In Vienna MS and editions this chapter begins with first sentence of chap. 14.

out violence or oppression, whence it can win great riches. Especially so, as trade is prohibited to the nobles, and they being magnificent and rich, the second estate by trade and by other means makes large profits from them.

To this estate also belong offices of finance which are great, very honorable, and profitable, and there are many of these of divers qualities, unnecessary to specify since they are well known. Although the other two estates are eligible for them, the offices of justice and of legal practice in France are nevertheless in the main in the hands of this middling estate, and this is a major matter both as to authority and to profit. For, in my opinion, France has more officers of justice, primary and accessory—advocates, procurators, clerks and so forth—than the whole rest of Christendom taken together.[32] Thence comes great and honorable maintenance for such folk of the middle estate as want to engage in other affairs than business. It seems indeed to some of the first estate that this second estate is better dealt with than their own. If the above-mentioned things are equitably maintained according to reason, however, each one ought to be contented with his estate and especially the first, which is always the greatest and most powerful, as well as the highest in dignity, so that men of the second always strive to attain to it, as I will show soon.

CHAPTER XVI
Of the Estate of the Lesser Folk [and Its Maintenance]

The vocation of the third estate, that of the lesser folk, is principally the cultivation of the land, the mechanical arts,

32. Aristotle *Politics* 4. 15. 1299[a]32. Cf. Roland Mousnier, *La Venalité des offices sous Henri IV et Louis XIII* (Rouen, 1945), and Ferdinand Lot and Robert Fawtier, *Histoire des institutions françaises au moyen âge* (Paris, 1958), 2:332ff, as well as the works cited above, n. 21; and on financial offices see Martin Wolfe, *The Fiscal System of Renaissance France* (New Haven, 1972), and Doucet, *Les Institutions de la France*, 2:551.

and other inferior crafts. So it is expedient that they be not in too great liberty or immeasurably rich and especially not generally trained in the use of arms. Otherwise, on account of their great number and their natural desire to attain [liberty and] a higher station, seeing themselves at the bottom, they might easily rise against the other two; and, if rich and warlike, they would trample down the other estates, should they undertake to do it. This has several times taken place in parts of this realm and several others.[33] In all lands in the world there are such distinctions of people [especially in monarchies], and this is necessary according to natural and political reason, just as in a human body it is necessary that there be inferior members serving the superior and more excellent. Nevertheless, in France this estate also has its liberties well maintained through justice, as I will show later; and as the other two are, so it is capable of several offices and charges—the lower offices of justice and finance, some lower ranks of military service in the army, and petty trade.

CHAPTER XVII
*How Men Go from the Third Estate to the Second
and from the Second to the First*

Moreover, everyone in this last estate can attain to the second by virtue and by diligence without any assistance of grace or privilege. This is not so in going from the second to the first, for to attain to the estate of nobility one must secure grace and privilege from the prince, who renders it readily enough when he who asks it has done or is about to do some great service to the commonwealth.[34] Indeed, the prince must do

33. The Jacquerie of the 1350s and later such uprisings.
34. Comprehensive and generalized views of classes and social mobility appear in Bridge, *France in 1515*, chap. 37, and Lewis, *Later Medieval France*,

this whenever there is legitimate reason in order to maintain the estate of nobility. This estate is always being depleted because in the wars in which it engages great numbers are often killed and because some nobles become so impoverished that they cannot maintain that estate. He must do it also to give to those of the middling estate the hope of arriving at the estate of nobility and the will to do so by doing virtuous [and difficult] deeds, and to those of the innumerable popular estate the hope of attaining to the middling and through the middling of then mounting to the first. This hope makes every man satisfied with his estate and gives him no occasion to conspire against the others, knowing that by good and rightful means he himself can attain to them and that it would be dangerous for him to seek to make his way by any other route. If, on the other hand, there were no hope of mounting from one to the other or if it were too difficult, overbold men could induce others of the same estate to conspire against the other two. Here, however, it is so easy that daily we see men of the popular estate ascend by degrees, some to nobility and innumerable to the middling estate. The Romans always maintained this same order, for from the common people one rose to that of the knights and from that of the knights to that of senators and patricians.

CHAPTER XVIII
How the Estate of the Church Is Common to the Other Three

In France the church offers another means, common to all the estates, for attaining to a high and worthy station. In this matter the practice in France is and has always been that by

---

chap. 3, with further bibliography; recent contributions to the newer social history are hardly relevant to Seyssel's level of interest or even perception.

virtue and knowledge those of the two lesser estates may attain to great ecclesiastical dignities as often as or more often than those of the first, even to the rank of cardinal and sometimes to the papacy. This is another great means to satisfy all the estates and to incite them to train themselves in virtue and learning.

For this reason I have always deemed it expedient and most necessary for the public utility of the realm, politically speaking, that the form of provision to the dignities and other ecclesiastical benefices by elections and ordinary provisions and nominations should be maintained in France, provided that it be used properly and according to the common law.[35] If things were done otherwise, all or most of the good benefices would find their way into the hands of ill-qualified men and by whatever means would be given over to the will of spiritual and temporal princes who would distribute them among their cronies and domestics, so that those who did not haunt the court of Rome or that of the king or were without acquaintance there would have very few of them. I do not say, however, that in the application of the law called the Pragmatic Sanction in France there cannot be excesses and abuses against the apostolic authority, nor do I wish to pass judgment on whether it is good and maintainable or not, for that is not my affair, but I speak of it, as is said, for the common good of the realm, and according to political reason. To avoid all scruples, I deeply wish that there were some *modus vivendi* in this matter useful and honorable to the king and the realm and agreeable, also, to the Holy See. This would not be too hard to find if pains were taken, but in order to get back to the subject, I will leave this to another time.

35. The Concordat of Bologna about to be settled, in Isambert, vol. 12, no. 18; cf. Jules Thomas, *Le Concordat de 1516* (Paris, 1910), and R. J. Knecht, "The Concordat of 1516: A Reassessment," in *Government in Reformation Europe*, ed. Henry J. Cohn (New York, 1971), pp. 91–112. In Vienna MS the last clause starts chap. 19.

CHAPTER XIX
Of the Harmony and Agreement of the Three Estates

All the foresaid things show the great order and harmony existing in all the estates of the realm, whence come the accord and unity of the kingdom, which cause it to be maintained, and preserved, and even increased daily.[36] Although these things are found in part in some other monarchies, nevertheless they are not found so completely, and all together.

If one of the estates falls into disorder the remedies are easier here than anywhere else. If the estate of the nobility, which has arms, seeks to outrage one of the other two en masse or individually, judicial power prevents it and chastizes the nobility. By consent of the prince, who does not refuse when necessary, this judicial power has authority to resort to force against rebels, so that there is none so great, strong prince or other, who is not constrained to obey. Likewise, if the popular estate, which is the largest in number, wishes to rebel, as it has done formerly, the nobility is so strong, along with the judicial power, and those people so feeble in feats of arms, that they can be easily brought to order and restored to their duty. Thus, because it is dealt with in such a way that it has reason to be content and because it recognizes that if it wished to exceed its bounds it could not well do so and would place itself in too great jeopardy, each estate keeps within its limits. In this way the estates think only to live in good order,* in concord one with another, and especially in obedience to the king whom for this reason all subjects hold in singular love and reverence. Whence it comes about that they are always ready to take up arms when necessary and to contribute to the needed *tailles* and *aides*.[37] In all other things the king is obeyed and served

---

36. Cf. Aristotle *Politics* 4. 11. 1295^{b}2.
37. Doucet, *Les Institutions de la France*, 2:557ff.

with good will, without opposition, and better and more promptly than any other prince on earth. If some particular disobedience takes place the remedies are so prompt and so easy that no great inconvenience or scandal results.

This suffices for this first part of our treatise, which is to show that the French Monarchy is better established to last long and prosper greatly than any other state or empire ever known.

SECOND PART
*The Things Necessary for the Preservation and Augmentation of the Monarchy of France by Means of the Polity**

There remains now the second section, harder to work out and put into practice, but also very useful and necessary, which is to show the possible faults and flaws of this monarchy and to propose the remedies to correct them and thus render it as perfect and perpetual as human wisdom and the fragility and imperfection of earthly things allow.[1]

To do this one should have the advice of many wise men with long experience of the affairs of the world, especially those of France, and it is not appropriate for one man, especially a foreigner, to speak of such matters too brashly. My zeal and obligation to the public weal of the realm, however, constrain me to write by way of introduction something of what I conceived in my own mind while I was in this realm and dealt with some of its great affairs at various times and places. This can do no harm nor prejudice and might, one hopes, be profitable in some instances, always remitting the whole thing to the correction of men of better understanding.

1. Aristotle *Politics* 5. 10. 1310^{b}39; cf. 2. 12. 1373^{b}27.

CHAPTER II

*Of the Education and Instruction of Princes
and Monarchs in General*

Since in this monarchic state everything depends on the
monarch, it seems that if the monarch be good [and wise] no
other remedies are needed to correct abuses nor other means
to have the polity* well maintained. Having the complete
obedience of his subjects, he can easily have the good laws,
ordinances, and customs obeyed and kept, can correct and
annul the useless or obsolete ones, and can make new ones,
if it is expedient. For the rest, by living in good order* himself he can induce his subjects to live well by his example. By
showing concern about the public welfare and being as
careful to understand it as those who have charge of it under
him, he can [easily] make them steer the right course. And by
remunerating the good and punishing the guilty he can inspire each one according to his estate and position with the
wish to show himself a man of good will and with the fear of
doing wrong and being held an evil-doer.

Of course, if the monarch always had sense, experience,
and prudence, accompanied by good will, nothing else
would be necessary, for that counts above all else. It is difficult, however, to find princes or other [mortals] sufficiently
endowed with all those qualities; and if someone were found
who had most of them, they would not likely be continued in
his successors.[2] Moreover, those qualities and virtues consist
in their practice and operation, without which they cannot

2. Aristotle *Politics* 3. 15. 1289^{b}22. Aristotle's own *Protrepticus* survives
only in fragments (on which see Werner Jaeger, *Aristotle*, trans. R. Robinson
[Oxford, 1934], chap. 4), but Seyssel knew the pseudo-Aristotelian *Secretum
Secretorum*, purportedly a letter to Alexander, available in the royal library at
Blois: see Henri Omont, *Anciens Inventaires et Catalogues de la Bibliothèque
Nationale* (Paris, 1908), vol. 1 (hereafter cited as Omont), publishing the 1518
répertoire of Guillaume Petit (Bibliothèque Nationale, Manuscrits, Fonds
français, vol. 2548), of which no. 106 is "l'histoire de Aristote, envoyee au
roy Alexandre."

be known [or realized]. It is necessary to descend to more detailed instruction and to teach precisely how the leader ought to conduct himself in all matters, as Aristotle did formerly for King Alexander [and as other wise and experienced men did for the princes of their times.]

Of the rearing and upbringing of princes in general, the virtues and traits that they should have, and the way that they ought to live and proceed in all affairs, so many good and notable persons have written in Greek and Latin and even in French [and other vernacular languages] that it would be superfluous to make a collection of them and rash to wish to add anything, since a new mode of presentation not employed by someone else would be hard to find. Some writers—Aristotle, Zenocrates [i.e., Isocrates—Ed.] writing to Neocles, king of Cyprus, and the glorious doctors of the holy church, Thomas Aquinas, Egidius of Rome, and several others—wrote treatises.[3] Others wrote in the form of history as did Xenophon in his book entitled the *Cyropaedia*, in which he described the traits and deeds of King Cyrus, not as they were in truth but as they should be in a wise and accomplished king.[4] Others adopted the style of orations and harangues, as did Cicero in the oration in praise of Pompey, and Pliny the orator in his panegyric in praise of the Emperor

3. Isocrates (= Zenocrates), *To Nicocles*; Aquinas, *De Regimine Principum*, in *Opuscula minora*, ed. Mandonnet (Paris, 1927), pp. 312–487; Egidio Romano, *De Regimine Principum*, in 13th-century French version, *Li Livres du gouvernement des rois*, ed. E. P. Molnaer (New York, 1899). In general, see Lester K. Born's introduction to Erasmus, *Education of a Christian Prince* (New York, 1936); Allan H. Gilbert, *Machiavelli's "Prince" and its Forerunners* (Durham, 1938); Wilhelm Berges, *Die Fürstenspiegel des hohen und späten Mittelalters* (Stuttgart, 1952); and Claude Bontems et al., *"Le Prince" dans la France des XVIe et XVIIe siècles* (Paris, 1965). Cf. Thomas More's discussion of counsel in *Utopia* in the Yale edition of *The Complete Works* (New Haven, 1965), pp. 94ff, and the introductions by the editors, Edward Surtz and J. H. Hexter.

4. Xenophon, *Cyropaedia*; cf. Machiavelli, *The Prince*, chap. 14, recommending the reading of Xenophon.

Trajan, and many others.[5] Even in French there are found *Spectacles of Princes* and other discourses in prose as well as rhyme, which are not to be scoffed at.[6] Others, in writing the histories of princes and narrating their lives and deeds, explain in what they are to be praised and imitated, and in what they are to be blamed and their example shunned. From all the histories that he knew of in his time, both Roman and others, Valerius Maximus has gathered the virtues and praiseworthy deeds of princes and great persons of Rome and foreign nations and also all their notable and reprehensible vices.[7] If a prince wished to take the pains and improve himself by frequently reading such books or having them read to him, and if he were well to weigh, retain, and take to heart the good teachings found in them, surely he would be perfect and he could not be given better teaching.

But, as I said, this instruction is hard to retain because of the prolixity of the treatises, and still harder to practice because of their innumerable teachings and examples and because of the fragility and imperfection of human nature. This is especially true with respect to men of high degree who, if wise and virtuous, are ordinarily occupied with great affairs, so that they scarcely have leisure time to spend on reading lengthy writings, or if young and willful are given over to lewdness and other vain and voluptuous actions.

To limit demand on their time and thus to avoid distracting too much those burdened with public affairs and boring those who scarcely wish to pay heed, I will limit my-

---

5. Cicero *Pro Lege Manilia*, trans. H. Grose Hodge (London, 1927), pp. 14–83, and Pliny *Panegyricus*.

6. "Les lunettes des princes par Jehan Meschinot," no. 154, Petit *répertoire*, in Omont. Among other relevant titles (not always identifiable) are no. 1, "Instruction au duc Charles de Bourbon"; no. 96, "Gilles de Romme, du Regime des Princes"; no. 105, "Gouvernement des roys et princes"; no. 109, "Xenophon, Histoire de Cyrus"; nos. 119–20, "Instruction d'un jeune prince . . ."; and copies of various works by Seyssel himself.

7. Valerius Maximus, *Factorum ac dictorum memorabilium*, one edition of which was by Guillaume Petit (Paris, 1513).

self to things that I deem most necessary to the government of the realm of France, presupposing that the present monarch is moreover endowed with gifts of nature and grace, so that he has the intelligence to understand what he must do and the will to do it. Considering his age, he has had enough experience and read diligently enough to know what he should do and desire and what he ought to flee and avoid. God, on whom all good depends and in Whose Hand is the heart of princes, knowing the king's good will, will direct him to all that is for the best both for himself and for his realm.

CHAPTER III
Instruction and Particular Introduction for the King of France

To come, then, in a few words to what seems most necessary for the maintenance and increase of this monarchy at present, speaking always in general terms, I will touch on several points which call for special attention because it has been observed during the lives of those still living that on them hangs the good or the ill, the prosperity or the misery of the realm. Chief attention must be given to those points, without going on to others, that come under the general head of good polity.* This is what doctors do when they recognize a dangerous tendency in a patient to fall into a particular sickness or indisposition; they put him under a regimen for that sickness alone, regardless of the ordinary regimen that should be followed to maintain general physical well-being.

CHAPTER IV
How the Prince Should Have Three Kinds of Counsel for Affairs of State, Aside from Those of Justice

First and foremost it must be kept clearly in mind that there is one fundamental necessity transcending all others in every monarchical regime. It is that the monarch do nothing by disordered and sudden will, but in all actions and especially those concerning the state that he use counsel, as all the wisest princes of the world have done in all important matters. Indeed God Himself ordered Moses to have counsellors, that is to say, the wisest and best renowned from among all the houses of His people.[8] It is scarcely possible for a single man, or even a small number of men, however accomplished, to understand and manage all the affairs of so great a monarchy. The mass of great affairs clouds the understanding of those who try to overload themselves, and thus they have neither the wisdom nor the time to consider matters well and sufficently or to debate them rightly, whence springs all sorts of trouble. Thus matters are dealt with in a careless way without prevision of what is likely to happen in the future or even discussion of all that should be considered in the present.

Care, however, must be taken not to communicate essentially secret matters to too large an assembly, for what comes to the knowledge of many people is almost bound to become public. When a large number of people is called to discuss secret matters, there is sure to be present a group of men who because of their degree, condition, or dignity cannot be left out, whose opinions often are not very well grounded. Nevertheless, since one is proceeding by the advice of counsel it will seem that the most general and common opinion should be followed, yet it might often be the worse, because in a great assembly wise, experienced, and clear-sighted men are always in a minority.

It seems hard to hit on an adequate means of solving this problem; yet one must be chosen, as best can be, considering the conditions of the time, the matters in hand, and the quality of the persons. And to satisfy everybody it seems to me necessary that a great prince have [besides the officers of

8. Exod. 18:19–25.

ordinary justice in France—the Parlements and the Great Council] three kinds of councils [for the affairs and business of the state] just as our redeemer Jesus Christ had, according to whose example we ought to do all things as far as possible. For besides the twelve apostles He had first His great council, the seventy-two disciples.[9] He did not often assemble them, for He sent them into various places to preach and to carry out His commandments, but in several matters He spoke to them all together, apart and separate from the crowd. The second council was the twelve apostles, to whom He ordinarily communicated all secret affairs. The third comprised three of the twelve, St. Peter, St. John, and St. James, to whom he communicated the innermost matters and highest mysteries, such as that of the Transfiguration. These He summoned for the greatest works and affairs, as at the hour He prayed to God His Father to be spared the Passion which He saw at hand. Even among these three there was one to whom He revealed more great secrets than He did to the others, that is, to St. John the Evangelist, when he reclined on His bosom at the Last Supper.[10]

CHAPTER V

Of the First Council, Which Is Called General

First of all I say that the king should communicate the great and common affairs of the realm to a great council assembled from good and notable persons of divers estates, ecclesiastical as well as secular and of the long robe as well as the short robe, men qualified by their degree, estate, or office. In France this would include the princes of the blood, the bishops, the heads of departments, the chamberlains, the masters of requests, and the masters of the household who

9. Luke 10:1 and 17 (70 instead of 72 in some versions).
10. Matt. 17:1–9, and Mark 9:2–9.

are at court.[11] Moreover, depending on the importance of the business, the presidents [and principal counsellors] of the sovereign courts, absent prelates, and other notable persons known to be wise and experienced may be summoned. To avoid confusion and expense such absent persons are not and should not be summoned often, but only when something most extraordinary occurs, something of great consequence to the whole realm, such as undertaking a war [and new conquest], making laws and ordinances of broad scope concerning the general justice and order* of the realm, and other such matters. In such instances it is sometimes expedient to call a small number of the men of the cities and chief towns of the realm.

This gathering is not called an ordinary council. On the contrary, it is an occasional assembly which should not be undertaken except when the circumstances require it. The one composed of persons at court can be called the General Council or the Great Council of the prince. It can and should meet more frequently than the occasional assembly: that is to say, in all matters of great importance concerning the state of the king's household, the ceremonies to be kept in cases of consequence such as rarely arise, or in case of a dispute between great persons, or such other matters which need not be secret but should be proceeded in deliberately.

CHAPTER VI
Of the Second Council, Which Is Called Ordinary

The second council should be ordinary, sitting every day when business is great and urgent, as in time of war or at the

11. *Ordonnance* of 13 July 1498 in *Recueil général des anciennes lois françaises*, ed. Isambert et al. (Paris, 1821–33), vol. 11, no. 17 (hereafter cited as Isambert). On the counsels in general see Roland Mousnier, *Le Conseil du roi de Louis XII à la révolution* (Paris, 1970); Noël Valois, *Le Conseil du roi* (Paris, 1888); and the works cited in pt. 1, n. 21.

very least three days a week, even though there be no special business. For in a great monarchy new matters requiring consultation are bound to come up. If on occasion there is no new business, still the assembly is honorable for form's sake, and when such people assemble some good suggestion useful in the conduct of current or future affairs results. This council should be staffed by wise and experienced men and especially by those who are zealous for the public weal of the king and the realm. In selecting them regard should not be paid to high birth, office, or dignity, but only to virtue, experience, and prudence; for these qualities are not born with men; they must be acquired by practice. Offices, dignities, and charges are not always given according to virtue and merit, although they should be. If they were, there would be no need to seek out persons other than those holding such charges and dignities to staff this council. Since this is not the case, it is necessary in selecting the persons on whose good sense and advice the prince must rely to choose those fit to bear the burden and guide the chariot of the commonwealth without considering any other inconsequential qualifications. Moreover, the number ought not be excessive. Depending on the number available, twelve such men or ten or even fewer will suffice, both because this helps avoid confusion, and because, in any case, very few men today are adequate for such a charge [and for keeping secrets]. Arrangements must be worked out so that no men except those chosen will maneuver to enter the council any more than they would to enter the Council of Justice or the Parlements, and so that no new man be called to give his opinion or attend, unless it is necessary on account of the quality of some personage who shows up inopportunely or of some affair of which a man not belonging to the council has fuller knowledge than anyone else. Such things must not occur often or without great cause, for otherwise confusion would shortly ensue and importunate men would crowd into the council, who could not be got rid of. To maintain this order the prince always must superintend this matter. Or, to deal with it, if he himself cannot or will not take such continuous pains, he must have under him a presiding officer of such authority and prudence that the king can rely on him to take such pains and that others will hold him in reverence as much or more for his virtue than for his office. Nevertheless it is most necessary that the king often attend his council, especially for important business, and not be content to get a report of conclusions, because if he is not present to hear a matter debated he cannot understand the root of it by such a report. Moreover, in hearing his councillors give their opinion he becomes acquainted with their wisdom and prudence and thereby learns which of them he can best trust and make use of. It also gives them occasion to think more deeply of his affairs and to tend more strictly to business when they know that the prince is there observing and judging their knowledge and their tempers.

CHAPTER VII
Of the Third Council Called Secret

Besides this council the prince must have a small number of this same council—perhaps three or four, or a very few more, of whom the presiding officer is one and the others are those whom the prince believes the wisest, most experienced, and most faithful to him—with whom he communicates separately concerning current affairs before they are proposed to the ordinary council.[12] For certain matters may come up which, because of their importance and highly secret nature or because members of the council may be interested parties, he ought not to communicate to so great a number of people. Before the council assembles the prince must talk over with this small group, which may be called the secret council,

12. Cf. Aristotle *Politics* 3. 16. 1287^{b}8.

what matters should be proposed. He must do this both for the above reasons and because by understanding the matter and what those of this very small council think of it in the first place, the prince may better grasp what is said about it afterwards by his ordinary council and what to say of it himself. Moreover, after the ordinary council has reached a conclusion it is essential to have the opinion of the secret council separately. For something which would not be for the best may have been advised by the majority of the ordinary council. In this case, if the prince has heard the opinions and previously understood the advice of the secret council to be otherwise, or if he suspects that the common opinion is not the soundest one, he should not at the time make a decision but reserve it for further consideration. If after having debated with the secret council he finds it inexpedient to follow the common opinion of the ordinary council, he may tell them thereafter in another assembly the reasons that moved him to do otherwise, without condemning their opinions, if there is no obvious reason to do so. Indeed, if the matter need be kept very secret, he may take action without telling them anything until it is put into effect. He should not reject the majority opinion too often, however, or without clear and evident cause, for evils can follow from this course. Those of the ordinary council would have good cause to be discontent and lose heart to advise well should they find themselves checked at every turn. Therefore, in this matter the prince must show great equity and consideration not to give too much authority to the one and too little to the other.

CHAPTER VIII

Of the Authority and Reputation That the Prince Ought to Give to His Principal Servants

Especially no person whatever should be given so much credit and authority that others are not permitted to con-

tradict his opinions or argue his proposals before the prince
without fear of danger. For in so doing the prince would put
himself in subjection to the favored one and give him occasion falsely to estimate himself and to do in his particular
interest things prejudicial to the prince and to the commonwealth. No matter how wise and prudent he might be, it is
nevertheless very difficult for one possessing such great
authority to remain balanced and to use it reasonably. If a
prince by long experience is familiar with the sense, virtue,
[loyalty,] and prudence of one of his servants, however, he
should not lightly give credence to things said against him
nor easily lend ear to his detractors. When any report is
brought him against such a person, or any other in whom he
has faith, the king should tell its author plainly that unless
the report be true he will punish him as he deserves. After
taking into account the quality of the person charged and of
him who makes the charge, the spirit that may have moved
the latter, and the circumstances and character of the deed, if,
all things considered, the prince does not see the likelihood
of the charge, he should rebuff and reprimand the informer
sharply and warn the person of the charge without naming
the informer, in order to see how he refutes it. Nevertheless,
if the matter is important to his person or his state, he should
keep his eyes open without exhibiting distrust to the ac-
cused. If the accusation has some likelihood about it and the
accuser offers to prove it, he should not be rebuffed but required to verify his imputation. Otherwise the door would
be closed to everyone who wanted to give a warning for the
prince's profit or for the security of his person or his state.
Just as a too-ready confidence in such informers would imply
light-mindedness, and thus wicked men would be encour-
aged to make a trade of acting as informers, so also would it
be imprudent to close one's ears to all accusers. Therefore in
this as in all things the middle way must be held to as much
as possible, and in showing that he has confidence in those

who manage his most important affairs the prince should not make them so sure of themselves that they ever cease to fear being discovered and punished, regardless of their rank and authority, if they do wrong.

Above all he should not rely too much on one man. I do not say, however, that he cannot have someone familiar with him and above all others in his confidence with whom as with himself he privately shares his lesser domestic affairs and secrets which do not touch the state, and even shares matters of state, for he would be deprived of a great happiness if he could not do so. It would be a dangerous thing, however, for him to decide matters of great importance, especially matters of state, according to the opinion of one man. For it is impossible or very difficult to find one possessed of all the qualities he would need in order solely by his own good judgment to unravel the affairs of a realm. The wiser a man is the less willing he will be to bear such a burden unless appetite for authority blinds him. It is obvious that the prince does still worse if he seeks to manage such matters by his own wisdom alone.

I conclude that he ought not to keep any matter concerning his state, however secret it may be, to himself and not communicate it to a number of his most confidential and trusty servants. For having kept to himself something of importance which should not have been secret he would bear more blame than for having published it too widely. In any matter whatever concerning his state he should not be so free and favorable to any man as to promise him not to communicate it to any living person, because this will give boldness and occasion to some malicious people of perverse spirit to whisper in his ears such things as will give him much groundless worry or notions that will redound to his shame and injury. He should indeed have such knowledge and experience of those whom he chooses for his most secret and innermost servants that he can speak with them as with himself. Many great matters have been ruined for not having been secretly managed, and many good plans have remained unexecuted because those who had them in hand feared to be frank and open.

CHAPTER IX
How Council Should Be Secret [and the Means the Prince Should Use in Secret Matters]

In fact the main concern of a council, and especially in a council reduced to a small number, should be to keep things secret.[13] To achieve this, besides the general oath not to reveal what is treated in council taken by all councillors when they are inducted, the prince should often bring the point to his councillors' minds, especially in matters of great importance which must not be divulged. When he is informed that other people have learned of such matters, he must diligently try to find out how this happened, and after he has found out make an example to others of the one who has erred. Moreover, when the matter deliberated upon is such that if the decision is known it may prevent the execution, as in military affairs, the prince well may and should reserve his conclusions until after he has heard the opinion of everyone, and later act according to the wisest opinion, communicating his decision to no one if he fears that it will not be kept secret. I judge, however, that the surest way is always to communicate it to two or three of the most faithful, especially if the prince does not consider himself adequately experienced in the matter in question. In this regard he had better have too little assurance and confidence in his own knowledge than too much. This in effect is what seems to me should be said for the present concerning that part of the council which I esteem paramount and most necessary, for if it is well reg-

13. Cf. Thomas More, *Utopia*, pp. 26ff.

ulated and maintained, the state of so powerful a prince cannot be imperiled nor anything happen to him so adverse that
he cannot readily provide remedy for it. If the course above
indicated is held to, there can scarcely come about a situation
of great importance which has not been foreseen and the
remedy prepared. Then the prince and those who have
charge of his affairs will make provisions for it coolly and
with assurance without frightening or even burdening the
subjects, as he necessarily does if he has to deal with great
crises in haste and disorder for lack of having provided for
them and done so in time.

CHAPTER X
Some Particular Matters to Which the King and Monarch of
France Must Chiefly Pay Heed for the Preservation and Increase
of the Realm

Although for the management of all monarchic states what I
have said before could suffice were it well kept to, nevertheless, not to stop at generalities, and considering too that the
wisest and most experienced men always try to learn, and the
more they know the more they hold everything in doubt, I
will proceed further to make several disclosures of the course
that the monarch of France and those who have his affairs in
charge must take for the conservation and increase of the
state. This I divide in two parts: the one concerning the ordering* of the interior of the realm, the other concerning its
external security.

As to the first I hold it for a maxim that all natural things
are preserved by the same causes and means which created
and brought them to being.[14] Therefore, considering well
what I said at the beginning of this treatise in speaking of the
forms and means by which this monarchy was created, con-

14. Aristotle *Politics* 5. 8. 1307^{b}25.

served, and increased in the past, it should be an easy matter to preserve and increase it more and more by holding to the same methods. But nevertheless, considering that as to practice there are some points which need to be better and more particularly understood because they have been poorly handled formerly, I will deal with them in detail, speaking always in general terms.

CHAPTER XI
How [the King] Should Maintain the Three Bridles by Which the Absolute Power Is Regulated

First, as to the three bridles above mentioned by which the absolute power of the prince, called tyrannical when used against reason, is bridled and reduced to legality, and thereby reputed just, tolerable, and aristocratic, I say again that the king can do nothing more agreeable to God, more pleasing and profitable to his subjects, and more honorable and praiseworthy to himself than to maintain those three things by which he acquires the name of Good King, of Most Christian, of Father of the People,[15] of Well Beloved and all the other titles that a valiant and glorious prince can acquire. On the other hand, when he breaches the three limits and wishes to follow his disordered will he is reputed a wicked, cruel, and intolerable tyrant, whence he gains the hatred of God and his subjects.

CHAPTER XII
Of Religion

Inasmuch as in all good things the beginning should proceed from God and the end be ordained by Him, every good king

15. "Pater patriae," or "père du peuple," was a title bestowed on Louis XII in May 1506 (Isambert, vol. 11, p. 449).

should above all maintain that principal point of religion, and the king of France above all, both for the reasons of which I have spoken above and also because he is more obligated to God than any other prince on earth, knowing that he holds from Him that realm which among all living men is esteemed the most noble, the most powerful, the most excellent and complete in all things. In another treatise [on the felicity of the reign of the late King Louis XII] that I have written on this matter I have shown this and made it manifest by several clear arguments, so I do not wish to repeat it here.[16]

Moreover, his predecessors having acquired the name of Most Christian by holy and virtuous works and the zeal they always showed for the Christian religion, the king would be greatly to blame who behaved in the opposite way, and he could well know himself to have been forsaken by God and expect grave punishment from Him. The more so since, besides the temporal goods and honors which God has given the king, He has endowed him because of his dignity with spiritual grace, that is, to cure scrofula, which no pope nor prelate nor prince whatever can do by virtue of his dignity.[17] He must, therefore, acknowledge this power to be from God when he wishes to use it, and put himself in a state of grace, and perform this most worthy and excellent mystery in full humility and devotion, begging the Lord not to regard his sins but the merit of his ancestors. After he has performed this act he should render thanks to God devoutly. Moreover, he should perform it often, especially in view of the number and the need of the sick.

Secondly, he must seek to the limit of his power that the Christian faith be well and completely maintained in his realm and all heresies and sects reproved if not extirpated,

16. Seyssel, *Les Louenges du Roy Louis XIIe de ce nom* (Paris, 1508). On the role of religion cf. Machiavelli, *Prince*, chap. 18, and *Discourses* 1. 12.

17. Cf. Marc Bloch, *The Royal Touch*, trans. J. E. Anderson (London, 1973).

and finally, that the name of God, of our Redeemer, Jesus Christ, of the glorious Virgin Mary His Mother, of the holy Apostles, Martyrs, Confessors, and Virgins are honored, praised, and exalted as they should be, not blasphemed and disregarded as they generally are throughout the realm, to its great scandal.[18] If the king wishes to prosper in this world and reign in the other, he must make such hardhanded provision that he will abolish this wicked detestable vice, most displeasing to God and neither profitable nor pleasant to those who are sullied by it.

Thirdly, he must hold the Holy Apostolic See in singular honor and reverence, and aid and favor it in all reasonable things, for in so doing the kings of France have acquired the surname of Most Christian and gotten many great honors and dignities, and have prospered in whatever they have tried. In addition he must take care that the churches of his realm are maintained in their liberty as he swears at his coronation, and see to it that they are well served and that prelates and churchmen, secular as well as regular, live as they should, each one in his place.[19] If there is disorder, he must do his duty and have it corrected by higher authorities, of whom he is one. Briefly, doing his duty toward God, he should show his good will therein to the people both in the way indicated and by the exterior acts of devotion, very appropriate and necessary for all princes but especially for one called Most Christian and the first son of the church. For people such as princes and prelates, whose lives are an example to others, a good zealous heart is not enough, unless they see to it that the light of their works penetrates to those

18. "Ordonnance contre le Blaspheme," 9 March 1510 (Isambert, vol. 11, pp. 569–72) is one of a long (and continuing) line of legislation against blasphemy and heresy.

19. Coronation oath, in Isambert, supp. vol. (1875); cf. Roger Doucet, *Les Institutions de la France au XVIe siècle* (Paris, 1948), 2:87ff, and Percy Ernst Schramm, *Der König von Frankreich* (Weimar, 1939), 1:258, 263.

whom they have in charge, for everyone easily follows the
ways of his spiritual or temporal prince.

CHAPTER XIII
*How the Prince Should Behave toward Prelates and in the
Matter of Their Promotion*

I will speak of one thing that is ill heeded in France and
elsewhere. It is that particularly in spiritual matters, preserving his majesty, every king and prince, however great,
should hold churchmen in great honor and reverence and especially the prelates who have the administration of the sac-
raments and stand in the place of the apostles. Although the
contrary abuse of doing the opposite emanates perhaps from
the imperfection and scandalous life of some of these prelates
and churchmen, still the dignity itself is not therefore less,
nor less to be reverenced than the royal dignity is though the
king be wicked.[20] There has been enough abuse on both
sides. Princes are the less excusable in this matter since very
frequently they cause the promotion to these dignities of
persons at whose hands both the poor souls in their charge
and the whole ecclesiastical order afterwards suffer. Laymen
are scandalized thereby and even the princes who had them
promoted. This is one of the things in which those princes
most offend God and for which they are today least esteemed. If the princes, to serve their persons and pleasures,
seek the best and most experienced cooks, tailors, barbers,
grooms, huntsmen, falconers, and other such, and if the very
finest archers that they can find guard their bodies and in
war acquire or defend land for them, how will they render
their account to the Saviour if, in the office appointed for the

20. On *Dignitas non moritur* see Ernst Kantorowicz, *The King's Two Bodies* (Princeton, 1957), p. 383.

care of the souls which He redeemed with His precious
blood, and to save which He does all things in this world,
they select persons who instead of showing the road to
paradise show rather the road to hell, or indeed, if they are
not wicked and do not give evil example, lack the knowledge
to exercise their office? In truth it is quite certain, if we are
Christians and believe in the Gospel and Holy Writ, that it is
the worst mischief that can be done in this world, the more
so since from it come all the troubles of the church. Such
prelates make priests and curates of the same sort; the goods
of the church, ordained for works of mercy, are expended for
worldly and evil ends; and, what is worse, the law and faith
of God falls into derision.

CHAPTER XIV
*Of the Abuses of Prelates in Our Time and the Means
to Reform Them*

I do not want to avoid speaking of these abuses, although I
feel myself to be among the most unworthy. For the problem
is not to undo what is done nor to depose those in office, but
only as best one can to make them concern themselves with
their office, to remove cause for scandal and be careful about
it hereafter, and to give thought to the great evils which result not only to the flock of us unworthy prelates but to the
universal church. For but few among those whose task it is to
defend and reform the church know how or wish to do so, or
are fit to attend a general council or appear before the principal heads of the church, or remonstrate with it properly. A
group of such men, although not numerous, with the zeal,
the knowledge, the authority, and the virtues to do these
things undoubtedly would bring matters into far better order
than they are now, for the truth is always stronger when it is
well held forth and sustained, and God, who is the Sovereign

Truth, aids those who maintain it, as can be seen by many experiences both of the past and of recent memory.

I will say nothing more of this matter, knowing that I speak against myself, except that the truth is of such virtue that even today those who deny it in their works are nevertheless constrained to acknowledge and to confess it, if not with their voices, at least in the secrecy of their conscience.

Therefore, knowing my imperfection, together with that of many others, and the scant duty that I have done up to now in the charge given me, although I could have done something, [and like many others in this estate being obliged to confess my own error and guilt and those of others, I say frankly that] I see one of the greatest faults of the church to be that the prelates do not keep residence in their bishoprics but on the contrary, on divers pretexts often proceeding from ambition, follow the ecclesiastical and secular courts.[21] And to the small extent that I can remedy this, I will take pains to do so. I pray that to me as well as to all others who have similar charges, God may grant the grace to fulfill that which I know should be done and that He may put it into the heart of those with the power to reform the church to understand this and to work efficaciously for it, and may the thing begin with me. If the Most Christian king would have true zeal for it and the matter were managed by good ministers, a great blow could be struck for reform right now, for many others would assist in it, and we should believe that God would do the rest. This would be one of the most meritorious works that could be done nowadays, and the public weal of the realm would profit from it in particular and the whole of universal Christianity, not only as to spiritual goods but also as to temporal. For if those who should be intercessors with God for the people, to turn away His wrath and obtain His

21. The marginal correction of the Vienna MS, incorporated in printed editions, clears up the "rather obscure wording" given by Poujol and suggests Seyssel's growing anxieties about his forthcoming clerical charge.

grace, were to be of the purest life and example and more
agreeable to Him, there is no doubt that their prayers would
be more efficacious for the salvation of souls, and that therefore the worldly would amend their lives. Thus they would
also be more efficacious in obtaining peace and prosperity in
temporal affairs. As a result God's punishments would cease:
plague, war, poor harvests, and others which God sends us
for our sins. And many riches would remain in every
province, but especially in this realm, which now go to and
remain in Rome because of the ambition of our ecclesiastics
and the rapacity of the Roman Curia. [I do not mean to say,
however, that it is not most essential for the court of Rome
and those of other princes, especially great ones, to have
some prelates in their council to help manage the affairs of
their states and the good administration of justice and to defend ecclesiastical liberty. And pray God that there may be
some who have the zeal and the knowledge to do this and
that they may be given ample authority, for this redounds to
the great well-being of the whole republic, both spiritually
and temporally. Those who frequent the court with this intention are highly meritorious, provided that they perform
their duty to their church by an alternate, as the exigencies of
business require. I speak, however, of those who out of
covetousness of wealth or ambition for honors follow the
courts of princes without doing any considerable service
there, but rather create scandal. Up to now I myself have
been of this number for a long time.][22]

Thus it is with respect to this first and chief bridle on the
absolute power of the kings of France, which they ought not
only to endure gently but also strengthen with their power;
for thereby all wealth and all honors spiritual and temporal
come to them.

22. Another marginal revision in the Vienna MS that made its way into
the editions.

CHAPTER XV
*Of the Care and Attention That the King Should Have
to Do Justice in General*

[Kings should also strengthen the second bridle,] justice, for
this it is that makes princes reign and rule, and without it
realms have been called dens of thieves.[23] Since through
good laws and ancient custom very long preserved God has
been so gracious to this most Christian realm as to have
given it the means to enforce justice with a greater authority
and rectitude than any other realm, surely the princes and
their subjects should try to maintain and strengthen it. After
religion it is the first and most worthy treasure by which this
realm is made illustrious, honored, preserved, and increased
above all others, and a monarch is the more bound to maintain and preserve it, as he is chosen by divine Providence to
this most great and honorable duty primarily to maintain
and do justice. This is the true office of princes, and therefore
there could be nothing more repugnant to his duty toward
God and his people than to violate, corrupt, or impede it. If
the officers under him who do not perform their offices to the
best of their power take their wages unworthily and are
bound to restitution in good conscience, as are the prelates
who do not perform their duties, so too are princes who do
not administer justice to the best of their ability. This is an
important matter and should be considered with respect to
God and conscience, which is of chief concern; but also, with
respect to this world and the universal good of the realm and
the king's particular good, it is the true pillar of the royal
authority. For by means of justice the prince is obeyed by all
alike, whereas if he uses force alone he must necessarily have
armies in every quarter of the realm. Yet violence could not

23. Augustine *City of God* (trans. M. Dods) 4.4: "Without justice what
are realms but great robber bands?"

have as much power as justice, for people naturally resist force and willingly obey [the ministers of] justice, as experience has always shown both in this realm and in others. The three estates of this realm are maintained and preserved thereby in true harmony among themselves and in true love and willing obedience to the prince. Moreover, this realm is celebrated and magnified throughout the whole world by reason of this great treasure of justice, wherefore the prince and monarch should study hard to maintain and increase it.

CHAPTER XVI
Concerning the Three Chief Things That the King Must Take Care for in the Matter of Justice

I could say many proper and necessary things on this subject, speaking especially of possible faults and abuses, since all things in this world are imperfect, but I will only speak of three which [more than others] concern the king. He must try to choose good and sufficient persons to administer justice. As he lacks the knowledge to recognize their sufficiency and fitness, where the choice is his, he must put the matter in charge of men who in obedience to the ordinance on the subject will make him a true and loyal report about it.[24] What is more, he should admonish the chancellor and other officers to whom because of their office this duty appertains to proceed in it according to God and their conscience, warn them that he will hold them responsible if afterwards they are found at fault, and do so indeed, should he discover that they have failed him. Surely, if he does this the justice of France cannot be ill, for there are so many good laws, customs, and ordinances that there only need be good ministers well to maintain and observe them, heeding nothing but the public weal.

24. See pt. 1, n. 22.

On the other hand, when those who should administer justice seek principally to enrich themselves, or out of ambition try to acquire friends more than to do right, or finally when they lack sufficient good sense and knowledge to do justice, it is as a fire and a poison to the realm. Thence come the laws' delays, superfluous expenses, and all the plundering, which are a wonderous burden in every land where this happens and are the more dangerous because the life, the honor, and the public repute of all other subjects is in the hands of the judiciary. Such is their power in France that they make and appoint and depose the prelates, great and small, under the color of the possessory power which usually closes the door to a process of appeal. Since the prince is responsible for the administration of justice, if he appoints men whom he knows to be wicked and insufficient, he is as responsible and chargeable for the wrongs and plundering that they do as any other officer is for the acts of his agent, and a merchant for the acts of his factor; so if he has God before his eyes he must take great care in this matter.

Moreover, because the offices are rarely vacant and those who hold them cannot be deposed without elaborate proceedings, the word and the exhortation of the prince would be very helpful in this matter. It would make those who hold office now or in the future behave properly if the king would often bring to the attention of the judges, especially of the sovereign courts, the complaints he has had concerning them, admonish them strictly to provide remedies and to do their duty, and grievously punish anyone found delinquent. It would also help if he would advance men of good renown, preferring them to honorable charges and bestowing rewards on them and their children, for surely that would inspire the wicked with greater fear and the good with greater hope than anything else. Especially the prince should take care that money does not change hands over appointments to these offices, as commonly occurs when they are made on the intercession of men not of the legal profession who have favor at court.[25]

Therefore, the prince should not lend an ear to such solic-itors, unless he is entirely certain that they are moved only by honest zeal. When judicial offices fall vacant it would be better if he secretly got information from men with the duty of making recommendations about the persons fit for such offices and then appointed them thereto without their re-quest or petition, as was done formerly on occasion. Thus all corruptions and shady practices would cease, and those appointed would not be obliged to any but the king. Other-wise, money must necessarily get involved or at least obliga-tions toward those responsible for advancing the appoint-ment, whence later arise many evils in the administration of justice, sufficiently manifest in this realm, so I will say no more about them.

Moreover, the monarch above all else must not sustain any party in the matter of justice on account of the affection he has for him; he must not promote the cause of any man above another or indeed in any suit declare his particular inclination with respect to any living man. His authority is so great and the virtue of men so small that such recom-mendations and declarations of affection made by a prince are almost bound to move the opinions of the judges, al-though they be men of honor and the prince protest in general terms that he only seeks justice. Especially in doubtful matters and in the sovereign courts where they judge rather by *epieikeia*, which they call equity, than by common and written reason, it takes little to incline a judge to an opinion, whence a number of evils often ensue.[26] By

25. On venality of offices, the *ordonnances* of March 1498 and 20 October 1508 (Isambert, vol. 11, nos. 26 and 85 and pt. 1, n.32.

26. The conception of equity, contrasted with the "written reason" (*ratio scripta*) of civil law, has been discussed by Guido Kisch, *Erasmus und die Jurisprudenz seiner Zeit* (Basel, 1960).

avoiding intervention, besides acquitting himself before God, the prince frees himself from being worked on and importuned to intervene in processes and matters of justice, which he will always be if he makes a habit of intervening. This applies principally to civil matters but is also pertinent to criminal cases in which, besides what I have said above, the prince must be most careful and show himself stern and reluctant to grant graces and remissions, especially in the case of wicked and detestable crimes so that it will be known that he abhors them and desires that they be punished. To this end when a petition is made for such criminals, unless there is extremely good cause for it he should censure those who make it, for in so doing he represses the temerity of the wicked and keeps all his subjects in awe, whereas in showing himself too easy to pardon and grant remissions he gives willful men clear occasion to do ill. I will not say more as to this point of justice, although there is much to say, except that the king of France should adopt all expedients indicated to him by the men of probity and means who desire the well-being of the realm to shorten the processes of justice. For people of all estates in this realm are ruined by the law's delays, and many whose right is good fail to prosecute it for fear that they cannot maintain the expense or prevail against special favor. So much for the second point concerning justice.

CHAPTER XVII

Of the Care and Regard That the King Should Have for the Police of the Realm in General

Since all that I will speak of hereafter deals with the third point, polity,* I will only say here that knowing that by means of the laws, ordinances, and praiseworthy customs of France concerning the polity* the realm has attained to its present glory, grandeur, and power and is preserved and maintained in peace, prosperity, and reputation, the king should watch over them and enforce their observance to the best of his ability, especially since he is bound to do so by the oath that he takes at his coronation. If he does otherwise he offends God, wounds his conscience, brings upon himself the hate and ill will of his people, enfeebles his power, and consequently diminishes his glory and renown.

Especially on this score he should carefully avoid alienating his domain, except in cases permitted by the laws and ordinances.[27] In doing otherwise, besides the evils mentioned above, he opens the door to the importunate, and once he has begun with one of them he will be pressed by many others who assume that they have merited as well of him as the first. If he refuses them they will become discontented, and envy will be engendered among his good servants; but if he closes the door and declares himself unwilling and unable to touch the domain, no one will have reason to be discontented nor the prince to be importuned.

To finish this item on polity* (which is very difficult to clarify) I must deal with the second point touched on in part one: the harmony of this monarchy of France achieved by the maintenance of the subjects of all estates in true accord to the satisfaction of each of them. Since the harmony thus achieved is the main cause of the preservation and augmentation of this monarchy, as is seen by experience, it is most important to maintain it and to prevent it from falling into disorder and discord, whence easily may follow the ruin of the monarchy and the dissolution of this mystical body.[28] To avoid this evil it is only necessary to maintain each estate in its liberties, privileges, and praiseworthy customs, and so to superintend all of them that one cannot lord it over the others

27. See pt. 1, n. 24.
28. See ibid., n. 7.

excessively nor all three join against the head and monarch. Because such things are better known by practice than by theory, however, and because past experience indicates several points as sources of great disorders in this monarchy, I will touch those points without going too deeply into particulars, except when the clarification of the problem requires it.

CHAPTER XVIII
How the King Should Maintain the Estate of Nobility in General

First, it is most essential that the king sustain and cherish the estate of the nobility (which is the first everywhere), not only by maintaining its rights and preeminences but further by showing all the people of this estate that he especially loves and esteems them, and has his main trust in them, and therefore desires their welfare and advancement. Indeed this is the dictate of reason, because theirs were the high and praiseworthy deeds whereby in the beginning the realm was established and afterwards augmented and preserved, and they have at all times defended it and are always ready to risk their lives in its defense. As reason demands, they have more love and reverence for the prince than any other estate, being better maintained in a higher and more honorable degree than the others, and moreover being of noble extraction and brought up to noble deeds, which should restrain them more than the others from base and cowardly acts.

In general I say that the men of this estate should always be preferred over those of every other in the honorable and profitable posts of which all the estates are capable, such as to benefices and offices of justice, providing they are equally adequate or even when there is some slight advantage on the other side, so long as the nobleman is personally well enough endowed with the qualities needed to administer the benefice or exercise the office. This quality of nobility merits some additional favor in temporal matters, be they ecclesiastical or profane, according to every human and divine law; but inadequate nobles should never be chosen because from this would follow all the troubles that I have spoken of above, and another besides which would redound to the damage of the estate itself. It is this: if the prince considered not the virtues and merits of the person but only lineage and favor, surely training in learning and virtue would vanish in this estate, and they would seek everything by favor alone, seeing that merely by this means they could attain to wealth. Understanding, however, that the prince sets greater store by merit and aptitude than by noble rank, each noble man would struggle to be known and reputed virtuous and capable of office.

This will be useful not only as to benefices and offices common to all estates but even as regards those belonging solely to the estate of the nobility, especially military offices. For among the nobility the quality of a man's house, his virtue, and his merits must receive recognition. In matters in which his choice is whole and free the prince must always prefer high merit in case of a notable difference between a man of a lesser and one of a greater house, preserving, however, to each one his dignity and prerogative.

CHAPTER XIX

How the Prince and Monarch, although He Protects the Estate of the Nobility in Its Preeminences, Must Take Care That It Does Not Become Too Insolent

The prince must carefully avoid giving this estate of the nobles so much authority, power, and liberty that it can oppress and outrage the other two, or one of them, or insult the prince himself, for thence rise very great disorders, as has often happened in this realm.[29] This the prince will do first and foremost by preserving his sovereignty and preeminence over all his subjects of whatever dignity, estate, or condition they be, preventing it as best he can from being lost or usurped in any manner whatsoever so that all will acknowledge him as natural and sovereign lord in all reasonable and customary matters. He should treat all men, moreover, with complete humanity, courtesy, and friendliness according to the estate and merit of each. He must not only maintain his authority and preeminence in what concerns his person, and the honor, reverence, and service due him, but also in what concerns his justice and sovereign jurisdiction. He should support the authority of the *baillis* and *sénéchaux* and other royal judges in cases and matters in which they have jurisdiction by law and custom over the immediate subjects of all princes, barons, lords, and other vassals whatever, as was most wisely established and instituted from earliest times and carefully maintained and observed, [and so must still be done]. For in truth this jurisdiction is one of the chief flowers of the crown. On the other hand, the sovereign should not in any manner whatever undertake or allow his officers to undertake any innovation against the rights and prerogatives of the princes, lords, barons, and vassals, except when he is clearly in the right and has taken good counsel in the matter, so that the subjects will not have just cause to complain. Anyone lightly giving credence to the royal officials would involve the majority of the nobility in litigation at every turn over the pretended rights of the king, whereby the nobles would be ruined because they would never recover the costs of the suit. In this matter the king must have great care and warn the officers who have charge of these causes that they should proceed as above indicated.

29. Most notably, the "war for the public good" (1465).

Secondly, the king should maintain equal justice for everyone, punishing crimes and delicts according to the requirements of the case without respect of persons except in some very special circumstance. He should show reluctance to grant graces and remissions in cases involving such misdeeds and especially to the military, who are continually under arms and by their nature and calling ready for violence and accustomed to engage in it. If they are not rigorously restrained, they are sure to ride roughshod over the other estates. This rigor must be employed to a greater or lesser extent depending on the situation, the persons, the times, and the matters in hand, but never be discarded or relaxed. In this way men of all classes will always fear punishment if they offend. It is more needful to maintain this vigor in wartime than at any other, as I will show later in treating of military discipline.

Moreover, the ruler should be observant of the quality of the persons he is acquainted with, such as princes and other great lords, and not give office or authority which they may abuse against his authority to those whom he knows to be of a seditious or arrogant disposition. For force and authority having come easily into their hands, such persons, out of pride or spite or for some other reason, may do things that result in great scandal to the king, the realm, and even to themselves. When great persons are of known virtue and good will, however, they cannot be given too much authority, for they are best disposed to serve well and most readily obeyed by inferiors. Nevertheless the ruler should maintain them in such a way that others are beholden principally to him for favors, that the chief subordinates and officers under the princes and great lords depend mainly on him, and that the subjects from all parts and provinces of the realm have to have recourse to him in matters of great importance. Otherwise he might easily lose or decrease the subjects' love and reverence and thus give occasion to men, especially those great in their own right, or to their lieutenants and officers, to misuse their great offices and commissions and perhaps to consider worse deeds, depending on the time and events; and if not to them then to those who succeeded them in similar charges, as happened in the Roman Empire. In this matter I only mean to speak in general terms and with regard to the future; for with respect to the leading men of our time one cannot and should not have any sinister suspicion; but my intention in this treatise is to deal with all things rather for the future than for the present, with primary regard for the prince's good and the preservation of the monarchy.

CHAPTER XX
How Care Must Be Taken That the Estate of the Nobility Be Not Impoverished by Men of the Other Estates

The prince must, moreover, take care not to give the other estates, especially the middling one, occasion to overwhelm and enfeeble the estate of the nobility so as to diminish its powers and wealth. Were the latter estate poor, it could not serve the king and the commonwealth in case of need. Among others, there are three main matters proceeding from the middling estate which impoverish the nobility. First, in the administration of justice the multiplication and delay of suits at law and the costs which must be met are such that every day the officers of justice acquire the inheritances and lordships of barons and noblemen, and these nobles fall into such poverty that they cannot maintain the estate of nobility but are constrained by dire need to do many things ill befitting their estate. Without doubt it would be very desirable to provide some remedy for this situation, which could easily be done, at least in good measure, if the king would put his mind to it, and if those to whom he committed the matter had as their chief concern the public weal of the realm. Of this I do not want to speak further nor enter into particulars; for it would serve no purpose if nothing were going to be done about it, and if anyone wanted to undertake it, the particulars would be easy to set forth.

What I have said of the offices of justice I say likewise of those of finance, for although it is essential that the persons who serve in them have great authority, administrative power, and obedience from the subjects in order that the exaction of the king's income may be more easy, nevertheless in all things there must be moderation and reason, and none should be given such authority and means to enrich and exhalt himself that others, especially men of a higher degree, suffer and are impoverished thereby.[30]

CHAPTER XXI
How Display Should Be Humbled

Care also must be taken that trade, the third calling of the people of the middling estate, does not destroy and impoverish the nobility. The sole cause of such impoverishment is the great displays that the nobility want to engage in and maintain and the excessive outlays that they make on their food and on everything else. But their outlay on clothes and other luxuries is the most pernicious of all, both to themselves and to the commonwealth of the realm, for thereby money goes out of the kingdom in great quantity. This is the worst evil that can be done to the kingdom, because money is its blood and nerves.[31]

Therefore the king can do nothing more useful for the

30. See pt. 1, n. 32.

31. Cf. Cicero *Pro Lege Manilia*, p. 7, "Vectigalia nervos esse republicae semper duximus;" and Machiavelli, *Discourses* 2. 10 (trans. A. Gilbert, *Machiavelli: The Chief Works* [Durham, 1965], 1:348): "Riches are not the sinews of war."

realm in a political way than to restrain these excesses of display, which besides their harmfulness are displeasing to God. Moreover, a whole group of other evils rise from them, for the king must give his very numerous servitors greater stipends or make them particular gifts in order to maintain this lavish display, or they would be ruined in his service. For this reason he has to tax the people more heavily. On the other hand, those gentlemen who have no stipend or benefice from the king, or only a little one, want to imitate completely or in part the style of the court. It could not happen otherwise, for never have the remainder of the subjects wanted to do anything but live according to the example of the princes and their courts. By this means the nobility is destroyed from lack of proper ordering* and thereafter cannot serve as needed but is forced to live ill. This is especially true of those who are in the regular cavalry, for there are more occasions for magnificence and festivities in this calling than in any other. Consequently men of probity and means, fearing this expense, which neither their wages nor their patrimony can maintain, withdraw, and in their place are put men of less worth and status who lay out in these mad expenditures a part of what they should spend to arm and mount themselves properly. In the end, unable to equip themselves suitably, they are constrained to pillage, as is notorious. No conceivable laws or ordinances will remedy this evil, unless they pulled it up by the roots, just as in the case of a sickness which stems from the evil humors of one member of the body. For although one may remove the pain partly and for a time by remedies applied to the aching part, still, unless the humors from which the sickness is born are purged, it will always begin again.

So, when all is said it would be expedient if, to put the whole thing in order, the prince began with himself and his court, as has been done in other times. In truth his fame and his repute does not at all consist in such display and elegance, but rather the greatness of the prince is diminished by them. For if he wished to go to great lengths in display, he could not be so well or richly dressed that it would not be a trifling matter considering his station; and men of little substance and sometimes of low birth would keep up with him and do as much or more. Therefore, in his person moderation tending toward little display will always be more esteemed than great magnificence, for extremes are vicious. I do not mean, however, that the outlay of the court should be so restrained as to make it shabby, for that would imply poverty in the realm; but only that moderation be observed there, and also that inferiors be made to observe decent order, for it is not reasonable that everyone be on a parity with the king or the princes or their chief servants. If good order were imposed in this matter by honorable and reasonable means without going to extremes, and if it were well enforced, it would be one of the best things that could be done to keep the realm rich and abundant in money, seeing that this is the leech which most draws blood from this mystical body.

CHAPTER XXII
How an Attempt Should Be Made to Increase the Flow of Trade and to Enrich the Realm

There is another matter pertaining principally to this middling estate and the practice of trade of which we are speaking. It is that neighboring countries have thoroughly observed laws and statutes to prevent gold and silver from going out of their lands and to draw to themselves the riches of foreigners. France does not do this, for if there are ordinances they are not enforced, and those who are supposed to enforce them often are the principal transgressors. If sometimes it is a matter of taking care not to discontent our neighbors (a care they do not take as regards this realm) under the pretext and for the fear that some calamity might follow from it, in fact it would not follow if we did to them as they do to others and nothing worse. It would be easier for us to do it, because this realm can get along much better without all the others than the others can get along without it.[32] But this monarchy is so big and cumbersome that to administer it is very hard, and it appears inexhaustibly rich and powerful in goods so that nothing seems able to exhaust it or harm it, whence comes most of the disorder. Therefore great merit and glory would redound to him who put everything in good order. If this were done in all things, or at least in those that I have mentioned above and will speak of below, I believe it absolutely certain that this monarchy would give law to all the powers and lordships of Christendom and even to several others, as I could demonstrate by reason and experience if I undertook to, but this is not the place to do it. Nor do I want to go into particulars about the means needed to prevent the outflow of money from this realm, for that is not my business, although I could say something about it. If anyone wishes to understand this matter he will find it easy to do, just as I said with respect to the multiplications and delays of legal process. And this will suffice for what pertains to the maintenance of two estates, that is to say the nobility and the rich [and middling] people.

CHAPTER XXIII
Of the Maintenance of the Popular Estate and How the Prince Should Relieve His People as Much as He Can from Tailles *and Impositions*

As to the lesser folk, the three principal means of preserving them can easily be understood from what has been said above, but nevertheless, because these means are of great

32. *Ordonnance* of 22 November 1506 (Isambert, vol. 11, no. 81 [= "80"]).

importance, they are worth repeating and explaining at this point.

The first is that the prince must be careful to burden these people as little as he can with fiscal exactions and do everything to [find every means to] make them realize that he deeply wishes to safeguard them to the best of his ability. In so doing he satisfies God and his conscience more than in anything else he may do; for he cannot raise large sums from the people without impoverishing a great number of them, indeed even depriving them of their meager necessities, for which their lament rises to God. It is this that must be the prince's chief concern, but besides, when he overburdens the people he brings on himself their hate and ill will, which can cause great mutiny and sedition, accompanied by adversity to the realm. Moreover, when the people are thus persecuted by exaction some are forced to leave the country. When a great number do so, it involves a large loss as well as ill fame and scandal, for in the countries to which they flee they spread rumors of the tyranny with which they were treated, and thus the indigence and poverty of the realm are revealed. The impoverished who stay behind desert the tillage of the soil and become beggars, both they and their children, which is another great evil.

Therefore the prince and those who have charge of his affairs should take great pains to restrain superfluous expenses which have to be met by such exactions. As to the method of levying such *tailles* and impositions, it would be well to moderate it somewhat and bring about a good reformation of it, for the money raised from the people by these means and under the color of these levies comes to a vast and incredible sum, far beyond what ultimately accrues to the profit of the prince. Many abuses, wrongs, and acts of violence are committed because of this exaction, whereby the officers deputed to make it—an infinite number—almost all enrich themselves, some greatly, others moderately, and all out of the blood and substance of the poor people.[33] I know, of course, that there must be officers to raise money and that it cannot be done without cost; but the excesses are so great, the abuses so manifest, that it is most necessary to make some provision against them, for the thing keeps going from bad to worse. And if the prince would give heed to the chief officers deputed in this matter and to others understanding it who are zealous for the commonwealth, they would willingly propose methods for a reform, which would be a great and meritorious act.

CHAPTER XXIV

How the People Should Be Protected from Oppression and from Pillage, Especially by the Military

The second point is that the people should be granted true justice so that those of the other two estates cannot oppress or commit outrages against them, as has been said above when speaking of the estate of the nobility. Especially the king and those who have the direction of wars under him ought to take care that the people are not trodden down by the troops. This is the main way to sustain the people. There have been many attempts to do it before, and yet sufficient order has not been taken or at least not kept. And so besides the oppression of the people, by this means so impoverished that they cannot afterwards bear the ordinary and extraordinary charges, there results a mortal hostility and hatred between the troops and the lower orders, sometimes so great that the people would be well pleased were the soldiers completely destroyed, which would be the ruin of the realm, as I will show at large hereafter.

33. Cf. Martin Wolfe, *The Fiscal System of Renaissance France* (New Haven, 1972), and John S. C. Bridge, *France in 1515*, vol. 5, *A History of France from the Death of Louis XI* (Oxford, 1936), chap. 32.

CHAPTER XXV

*How the People of Low Station Should Be Given Heart and Hope
to Attain Through Worth and Industry to a Higher Status*

The third point is to maintain the people in their freedom
and liberty of being able to engage in all occupations not
prohibited to them and especially those mentioned in the
first part of this treatise by which they can attain to a higher
status, that is, trade, learning, letters, and arms, according to
their station. If any of them show aptness in one of these
callings he should be helped and favored according to his
merit and promise, to give heart to others to emulate him in
hope of attaining what he has attained. This is the true spur
which makes all sorts of folk follow the road of merit, and one
individual who is raised in this way brings ten thousand to
follow him, as has been seen by experience at all times and is
recorded in a thousand places. Because there is a dearth of
worthy and able people in every estate and since it is they
who do the great services in all matters, the prince must indeed try by all means that he can, but especially by the one I
have spoken about, to arouse an appetite in his subjects of all
sorts to work to attain merit either in learning or the military
art (the two main ones) or in other active occupations such as
trade, navigation, law, or other such. Because this point and
the one preceding mention war and the condition of the military, which primarily ensure the power of the realm (although so closely linked with the polity* that the one cannot
be maintained and preserved without the other), I will now
deal with the might of the realm in general and particularly
with the arrangements* necessary to maintain and increase it
for the preservation of the realm and its expansion if need be.

Military Power and the Maintenance and Augmentation of the Realm Thereby

The power of the realm in my opinion consists mainly in four things, to wit: in the unity of the subjects in obedience to the prince, in their riches, in the valor and training in arms and warfare of those deputed and ordained to that calling, and in the power and provision of cities, towns, and castles, especially those at the borders and boundaries. All these things depend on good counsel and government. For this reason a wise man said that if there was not good counsel within, arms without were of little worth.[1]

In dealing, therefore, with these four points I will not say much about the first two because what I have said before is enough to show the way to maintain them.

CHAPTER II

Of the Fortification and Provision of Strongholds

Since the fourth point is obvious enough, I will only say that it is most essential, since a good town or stronghold, well provisioned with abundant artillery and stocked with ev-

1. Cf. Prov. 11:14, 15:22, 24:6.

erything necessary to sustain a seige, feed a garrison, and wait for succor, is the salvation of a whole realm, as experience has often shown and that of the recent past more than ever.[2] Therefore the prince should set himself to this task and support it with his revenues with the grant of certain reasonable impositions and with concessions of privilege for a limited time. Moreover, the inhabitants of such towns and places and those of the neighboring countryside who can withdraw to those towns and save themselves and their goods in time of war may in reasonable ways be constrained to make some contribution. Repairs and fortifications should be made in peaceful and quiet times, for thus the people will be less heavily charged and the work much better done. Then if a crisis does come, the people will not be overburdened or terrified, as they are when they have to make fortifications in haste, in which case what they do is neither sound nor durable. Because in all such matters great abuses are almost always perpetrated, to the oppression of the people and the loss of the prince and the commonwealth, the men in charge of the work must have a sharp eye and be most alert. And so they will be, if they are men of substance and probity, honorable, wise, experienced, and zealous for the public weal. Therefore the main thing is to give such tasks to men who know about them and want to perform them.

CHAPTER III
How the Prince Must Travel Through His Provinces

Nevertheless, as such persons are not always to be found, and in the long run each man's mind inclines to his own particular good, when the prince is not held back by great affairs elsewhere he must occasionally visit his lands, espe-

2. Referring perhaps to the siege of Ravenna, 8–11 April 1512, in which Gaston de Foix died and after which the French were helpless against the Holy League in Italy.

cially those on the frontier, in order to see how the work pro-
gresses, how the people are governed, and how the officials
are behaving themselves. He must give every indication of
being much concerned about these matters, granting audi-
ence readily and remedy promptly to subjects coming to him
with grievances. If he does this, besides acquainting himself
with the condition of his affairs he will give contentment to
his people and will win men's hearts much more than if they
know him only by his writs. Thus he will be held in awe by
his officials of every estate and kind, and by his captains and
others in charge of his army, if there are any in the area.
Besides, money is thus distributed throughout the realm and
especially in the places where it is most essential that the
people be well-to-do because they most frequently have to
bear the heaviest burdens.

CHAPTER IV
*Of the Army, and How It Is Essential That There Be an Infantry
Trained for War in the Realm, and How to Raise, Train and
Maintain It*

I return now to the third point about the armed force, which
has to do with the soldiers. To know how this matter should
be managed and to execute it in practice are both very difficult and very important. Although I have said that training
in arms was only for the nobility and that it was not expedient for the people to be habituated to them for fear of the
evils alleged above, it seems that we are faced with a great
perplexity here, for it is undeniable that those evils are to be
feared if the people are accustomed to combat. Given a favorable occasion and moment, they may become disobedient;
they may refuse to pay the customary charges; finally, they
may ruin the nobility. Reason and past experience both indicate these things.

On the other hand, many evils result if the people are not

accustomed to combat. If they are useless in war and some foreign nation attacks, the realm is much weakened for lack of an aggressive infantry, without which war cannot be waged, especially against the infantry of those the realm must fear most as enemies, to wit, the English, the Germans, and the Swiss. Whence it comes to pass that when the people hear of an attack from one of those nations, especially in parts where they are least combative and most unskilled in arms, they are frightened and terrified, however small the enemy band may be and however great their own number, even though they have the help of a good force of soldiers. The latter, seeing the fright and lack of heart of the people, cannot trust them at all and they themselves become fearful and worried, knowing that without the help of foot soldiers better than these they cannot very well repel the enemy nor sustain their attack. On the other hand, the enemy, knowing this, is more bold to undertake an assault on the king and his land and subjects, which is a great evil. Were so numerous a people combative, no neighbor or other power in the world would dare undertake to assail them. It is true that in case of need, by means of revenues that can be levied from the people, there can be raised from other nations a combative infantry which can be discharged when the war is over, the realm thereby resting free and discharged of such folk; whereas subjects so engaged stay in the country and do nothing but oppress and harm the people, as has been seen by past experience after the wars long waged in this realm. Nevertheless, to employ strangers in this situation has resulted and always may result in several other evils as much or more to be feared.[3]

In the first place, money that should remain in the realm goes out of it.

Secondly, the king cannot have such confidence in

3. Cf. Machiavelli, *The Art of War*, bk. 1.

foreigners, especially in people of low condition such as infantry ordinarily are, as he can have in his subjects. Also, one
cannot bring them to reason, or make them fight, except
when they want to, or make them be satisfied with their pay;
and in sum, one never has complete obedience from them.
Therefore it is impossible to make them maintain military
discipline and to have full faith in them. If they commit a
wrong, since they are very numerous, one cannot easily
punish them, and yet the fault could be such that it would
lose the whole game—a battle or a powerful town—whence
might follow the loss or destruction of a region or a part of
this realm. Besides, it might happen that these foreigners,
seeing that they have the upper hand, would make themselves lords and seize some part of the country, as has occurred several times in this realm and elsewhere.

Thirdly, it could come about that the foreigners to be used
would not or could not come to the help of the king as
quickly as need be, and meanwhile the enemy might do
some irreparable harm.

Fourthly, it is a very dangerous thing to draw bellicose
foreign nations into such a realm as this and accustom them
to it, for by long sojourns here they learn all its methods and
secrets of war and the condition and stratagems of its armed
force. They also see and become acquainted with its imperfections, with the feebleness of the people and the fortresses,
with the weaknesses of towns, castles, and passes, and, what
is worse, with the wealth and great riches of the realm—all
spurs to move them to come and wage war and invade it, as
has frequently happened in several other realms, regions,
lands, and lordships, and as has very recently happened
here.[4]

For these reasons and because old histories and recent

4. Referring perhaps to the Swiss invasion of 1513 (and the numerous
pillages by mercenary troops).

ones as well tell us that the empires, monarchies, and states which used too many foreigners in their wars were lost and destroyed thereby in the long run, I find it very dangerous for the people to be so useless for war that we should need to employ strangers. On the other hand, to use one's own people in war may result in other great ills. Therefore, in order to obviate all difficulties as best can be, it would seem good and necessary to put in execution a plan previously recommended, to wit: to establish a permanent infantry throughout the realm, choosing from every town and parish a certain small number of the men of the greatest vigor and readiness for war and of the best type available. They would have captains from the same region, who would know them and could be responsible for them if they committed any wrong. These captains would be of the infantry, men of honor who would not disgrace themselves by pillage, nor draw profit to themselves, nor out of favor give places to useless men, but would devote themselves chiefly to the service of the prince and the good of the republic and would above all keep the soldiers in order.[5]

The main leaders in war, such as the constable, the marshals, the lieutenants, and the governors of provinces, and others commissioned for this service, would have supervision over this infantry, that is, would have them trained in arms during peacetime and have several veteran foreign foot soldiers of highest expertness in war teach them the order and rules of fighting and all other things pertaining to that calling. Moreover, these supervisors and commissioners for taking the muster would inspect the persons, armor, arms, and equipment of the soldiers, take care that no fraud or deception was practiced, and see to it that all was done with the least possible hurt to the people, paying the soldiers sufficient wages in time of war and reasonable maintenance in

5. *Ordonnance* of 20 January 1514 in *Recueil général des anciennes lois françaises*, ed. Isambert et al. (Paris, 1821–33), vol. 12, no. 5, undertakes a reform of the *gens d'armes*.

times of peace. Nevertheless, if meantime any crisis occurred for the realm, before these men were tried and ready for war, whatever number of foreigners the situation required could be brought in, along with whom the local levies could serve.

Of course, when war was to be waged, in order to spare the native soldiers or to use soldiers of diverse kinds and higher military skill and to support some neighboring nation, some of the best and most reliable foreigners could be called on in great crises, but always in number less than the French. By this means all troubles would cease, because the foreigners would never be so powerful in the army that they could abuse the others or that they could not be brought to reason. Moreover, seeing that the realm was provided with good foot-fighters as well as cavalry (which is the best in the world), these strangers would be afraid not so much of assailing them as of being assailed by them, and in this way they would always live in complete amity with the king and his subjects and would refrain from offending them. The money which the infantry would be paid would remain in the realm, so the people would not be too greatly burdened. In this way there would be no danger in putting arms in the hands of the populace, because the number of such permanent infantry would be so small in each neighborhood that they could not stir the rest to mutiny, nor conspire together, being from so many different parts of the land, nor would they have occasion to do so, since they would be getting pay, liberty, and other preeminences above the other folk of their estate and would thus be more obedient and more fearful of insubordination. If help were needed in the execution of justice they would always be ready, so that it would not be necessary to raise other men to execute it by force. I do not say that at the boundaries of the realm and especially those on the frontiers of our most dangerous neighbors the people should not be permitted to be more warlike and better trained in arms than in those in inland places. On the contrary, the men in charge of such regions should offer the people inducements and provide the means, such as offering prizes for skill in the use of longbow, crossbow, and arquebus, and in combat with sword and pike, and other such military exercises, summoning for this purpose not all the inhabitants in general but those most apt and disposed to this calling. For people living at the frontiers must be armed and equipped, bold and trained, in order to resist neighbors who are all those things too. Otherwise they would always get the worst of it in all the conflicts rising over boundary disputes; or if other men, even though they were inhabitants of the kingdom, had to come to their aid, it would be most costly and burdensome for the frontier lands.

Such frontier people are usually better affected to the prince's cause than others are, because they have more often fought for it, and because for this reason they have been freely exempted from certain charges and impositions borne by people not living on the frontier. But besides the dangers they undergo in times of war they bear other burdens. For ordinarily they have a military garrison and are bound for watches and repairs of strongholds and towns.

There is one other point concerning the armed force, to wit, the navy, of which I will speak in the following part, where it is appropriate.

CHAPTER V
*Of Military Discipline, How Necessary It Is
and What It Consists Of*

The chief point in all these matters is that among the military, infantry as well as cavalry, in time of peace as well as in time of war, within the realm as well as without, the king must preserve military discipline which maintains order in all matters of war and from which all obedience and in fact all victories and good things derive. I will here touch on several points about it without quoting Valerius, Vegetius, or others who have written fully concerning these matters, for this would be too complicated a task.[6] I will deal only with what is relevant to the present time because we have had recent experience of it, to wit, the calamities resulting from lack of discipline and the remedies which can be applied in the future, remitting the rest to the prudence of the king and his principal military officers and also to what is to be found in books.

Of what efficacy discipline is is not unknown to any man acquainted with histories, especially those treating of the deeds of the Romans, who were of all others the most careful to preserve it. More than military power, it was the cause of the grandeur of their empire of old, as Valerius Maximus and several others bear witness. They narrate examples of Roman leaders and emperors who, having reduced their forces to that discipline, afterwards had victory over the same enemies that had formerly conquered and routed their armies when they lacked discipline. Among other examples that of Scipio Africanus in Spain is good evidence in proof of this. Therefore all princes and war leaders should try to preserve discipline; and to speak of it briefly according to my plan, I will say only that it is most necessary at this time for the French monarchy.

CHAPTER VI
What the Commander-in-Chief Should Be Like

Discipline consists in two things, of which one effectively depends on and proceeds from the other; they are the valor and adequacy of the leaders and the obedience of the soldiers. If the commander is what he should be and the officers and soldiers of all ranks obey him as they should, everything

6. Valerius Maximus (see pt. 2, n. 7, and Henri Omont, *Anciens Inventaires et Catalogues de la Bibliothèque Nationale* [Paris, 1908], nos. 1586–90) and Flavius Vegetius Renatus *De Rei Militari*.

will go along well; but when one of these two is lacking it is almost impossible that anything good be done. So if the commander does not through long experience know the military art well enough to order what is to be done in all cases, and lacks the valor and prudence to execute what has been planned, he will never win reputation or esteem among his men or among the enemy either. Whatever enterprise he undertakes, the soldiery will feel no confidence in it but will suffer fear and misgivings, whereas if they esteem him as they should, they will always have a good opinion and hope of everything that he undertakes and go briskly and boldly to work. What is worse, if he lacks heart or knowledge, he will often be surprised by his enemies and will not make opportune preparations on his side, and consequently he will commit a thousand errors, of which in warfare only one is necessary to lose a state. It is not enough to provide a commander unsuited to this office with counsel and assistance from able men of honor because the commander himself must have sense enough to understand the business and to judge among several different opinions which is the best. Otherwise he might easily choose the worst opinion, although that of the majority; the more so because when certain men have complete authority with the military commander, the others, ordinarily displeased because of this, out of envy contradict their opinions, whatever they say.

Besides, unduly young and inexperienced commanders often put too much trust in someone complaisant to their whims or in someone who has brought them up from childhood, although he knows nothing and is held in little esteem by those of greater knowledge. Moreover it is essential that the commander himself have good judgment and experience enough to command and execute on the spot actions which cannot await the deliberations of the council or even be communicated to it.

However good the advice the commander may get, if he

lacks the heart, the valor, or the prudence to know how to put it in execution by deed and word or even to make himself obeyed, the help of the wise profits him but little. In conclusion, we have seen so much trouble come through the failings of commanders selected by favor and without regard to the matter in hand that there is not a man living whose mouth and ears are not full of it. Therefore, if commanders with all these qualities and parts were to be found, beyond doubt they should be preferred to all others and bought for their weight in gold. Nor would a prince or anyone else refuse or take it in bad grace to be subordinate to such men, if they had the complete authority of their master, as is necessary and as I will indicate hereafter. Because such are rarely to be found and one must cut one's coat to fit one's cloth, the king must choose the least imperfect from among those available, looking for the most essential qualities and traits and selecting the man who has most of them. Above I have spoken of the three traits that Cicero mentions in his first oration for Pompey.[7] To these he adds a fourth, good luck, at which I did not choose to pause because it follows from the others and in the long run scarcely can exist without them. And I say the same about authority, for whoever has the other two qualities—knowledgeable experience of the craft and valor—will always have authority and reputation if the prince treats him as he should.

CHAPTER VII
Which of the Two Qualities, Valor or Knowledge of the Craft, Is Most Essential in a Commander

Therefore we must consider which of the two traits, knowledge or valor, is to be preferred, if a man is found having one

7. Cicero *Pro Lege Manilia*, p. 40; 14. 47.

and lacking the other. I mean if the lack is quite notable, for a man who has one quality completely and the other in some measure is always to be preferred to him who is clearly deficient in one. Thus the question rises when there are two commanders equally qualified, one in one quality, the other in the other. From the order Cicero follows in the oration mentioned above, it seems that he prefers knowledge of the craft to valor. Nevertheless, it seems that valor is much more essential, for with that much more can be done by good advice than knowledge without valor can do. This was the case with Alexander, Hannibal, and Scipio, all three of whom were leaders so young that they could not have had sufficient knowledge or experience, but by means of their valor and courage they did greater things than many others long trained and experienced in arms, who lacked their stoutheartedness.

In my opinion, if one trait and quality were totally separated from the other, that is to say, if there was a man perfect in the art and experience of war but with very little heart and another who had a great endowment of valor and little or no experience in war, I would choose the latter rather than the former, both for the reason indicated above and also because he may easily improve himself by training. This the former can never do, especially since after so long a career in arms in which he learned the art adequately he did not attain courage. But because it is hard, indeed almost impossible, that a man long engaged in the profession of arms and fully understanding it should lack sufficient courage, whereas many have a valiant heart by nature but no training in arms or knowledge of the profession, I think that this moved Cicero to put knowledge of the art as the first and most essential quality for a war leader. If this is the case, one may assent to his opinion.

CHAPTER VIII

*In What Case a Prince or Other Great Person Should Be Preferred
to an Important Post over a Lesser Man and How Essential It Is
That a War Commander Be Eloquent and Harangue His Soldiers*

Personal rank or preeminence is very helpful to a leader in
obtaining the obedience, love, and esteem of military men.
Therefore if princes or other leading persons of the realm
have enough of the previously discussed qualities, and especially of valor, they should be preferred above all others,
even those more accomplished, provided always that courage is not so linked to rashness that it underrates the advice
of the wisest and most experienced men. If it is so linked, the
greater the man is, the greater the disorder he will cause. But
if he is cool and deliberate enough to heed gladly the opinion
of those whom he knows to be adept in the profession, and
had enough sense to judge well after he has heard matters
debated, and enough valor in execution, I believe that under
such circumstances he should be preferred above any other
man and be assisted by subordinates who can supply those
things in which he is deficient. What I say concerning a
commander in the prince's absence should all the more be
held to when the prince himself is engaged in the war, for it
is not permissible that there be any leaders not subordinate
to him. Therefore, if he lacks experience in arms, he should
not for the world do anything important about them without
the advice and counsel of men more knowledgeable and experienced. Even if he have adequate experience still he
should take counsel, depending on the importance of the
business and the situation at the time, just as has been said
above as regards affairs of state.

Another quality seems to me most essential for a commander, to which no heed is given in France, that is, that he
be eloquent and acquainted with many ancient and modern

histories.[8] For in a crisis the wise remonstrance of a leader, soundly based on good reason and good examples, much strengthens the heart of a whole army to the point of making the soldiers as brave as lions, where before they were as terrified as sheep, as can be seen in several passages of Caesar's *Commentaries,* especially when at Besançon he wished to join battle with Ariovistus.[9] And whoever has read Xenophon's history of the journey of Cyrus in Persia [which I have translated from Greek to French][10] will find there other and more clear-cut examples and also in Sallust, Titus Livius, Quintus Curtius, and all other historians. Therefore it seems to me that if this method of haranguing the military in great crises were restored, and if those whose business it was knew how to do it properly, it might be most useful. So much for the qualities and traits that the lieutenant of the king who is in command during a war ought to have.[11]

CHAPTER IX

Of the Power and Authority That the Prince Should Give to a Commander-in-Chief

On the part of the king and sovereign something else is essential. It is, having chosen a man adequate to such a charge, to give him complete authority in what concerns the waging of war, so that there will be none so great under his command as not to be constrained to obey him as they would the king in person. The latter must not lend an ear to any man whatever who is unwilling to obey his lieutenant, and the

8. Cf. Machiavelli, *Art of War*, 660, and *The Prince*, chap. 14.

9. Caesar *The Gallic Wars* 1. 3841; Xenophon *Anabasis* 3. 2. 7–32; Sallust, *The War with Cataline,* trans. J. Rolf (London, 1931), pp. 118–23; Livy 28. 25–29; Quintus Curtius 3. 10; 6. 3; 10. 2–12.

10. See introduction, n. 19.

11. In Vienna MS and editions this sentence begins chap. 9.

greater the person unwilling to obey the greater the punishment he merits, because such a one will draw many others
after him. If, as had been said above, the commander is not
esteemed, feared, and obeyed he cannot possibly do anything worthy.

For this reason, I have also said above, speaking of the
state of the Venetians, that they are not to be praised for
having over the leader other men who can lay down the law
to him concerning the waging of war, ordering him to give
battle, to besiege or relieve strongholds, to break or promote
men, to take towns by force or by treaty, to punish those
slack in arms, to reward those who merit it in transient or
unimportant matters, to depute captains to the towns and
other strongholds in his command during the war, and other
such matters.[12] Especially he ought not have for superiors or
associates people not knowledgeable in the art of war, whatever their social quality and authority may be. I do not say
that in matters of policy,* justice, and finance, not strictly
military, it may not be necessary to have other people to
manage them, both to avoid busying the commanders with
so many other matters that they cannot fulfill their function
and also because these are different kinds of office, and he
who is apt for one is not so for the other. Moreover, it is
inexpedient to give so much authority to one man, officer,
and subject that he need not have recourse to the prince in
matters of great importance which do not require immediate
action. Especially, a leader must not have authority to begin
a new war or to make a peace or a treaty for a long period
with enemies or other foreigners without the permission of
the princes, except in cases of necessity, which is reserved in
all matters. Finally, to be brief, care must always be taken to
give more or less authority depending on the quality of the
person, the matters in hand, and the distance of the places

12. See pt. 1, chap. 3; and cf. Machiavelli, *Art of War*, 586.

involved. Thus did the Romans, who gave greater authority
to the consuls they sent to distant regions than to those who
stayed in Italy, and more to some by reason of their merit and
reputation than to others. In extreme necessity they created
the dictator who had total authority. This will suffice on the
matter of the commander insofar as it consorts with our purpose and haste. And anyone who wants a fuller and more
minute account of the traits and merits that a commander
should have, the course he ought to follow, and the matters
pertaining to his office, can find long treatises about it and
learn of it in the discourses of many historians noting what
has been told of those of the highest renown such as Cyrus,
Alexander, Pyrrhus, Hannibal, Marcellus, Fabius, Scipio,
Themistocles, Lysander, Caesar, and other princes, dukes,
and emperors, [such as those described by Plutarch].[13]

CHAPTER X
What Military Discipline for Soldiers Consists In

Amply set forth in those treatises and histories we also find
what is appropriate for the military discipline of soldiers,
which is the second point I want to speak of. Although discipline entirely depends on the matter just dealt with, to understand it better I will treat this aspect separately, and will
only say that it seems to me especially necessary at present
among the French cavalry troops, to judge by what I have
seen and heard about them from leaders who understand the
profession. There are three main points generally affecting
military discipline.

First and most necessary is the obedience of the soldiers
to the commander, about which we have said enough above.

---

13. Sertus Julius Frontinus *The Strategema* 4; Cornelius Nepos, *The Book
on the Great Generals of Foreign Nations*; and Plutarch.

There remains nothing more to say except what Scipio Africanus observed: "Better a thousand obedient men than ten thousand disobedient." This obedience depends on the commander, for if he is such as we have spoken of, and the sovereign gives him the authority he should, he undoubtedly will get obedience because no nation of people is so unbridled that they cannot be brought to reason by justice. Justice is more necessary in war than in any other situation, because without it no order can be maintained, whence comes all sorts of troubles which are most unfortunate in such affairs. Therefore those leaders are very blameworthy who, to acquire the affection of the army men or to show themselves gracious and good-natured, are too ready to pardon or cover over the faults of the soldiers, especially where disobedience to the commander or his ordinances is involved, because from this proceeds the complete dissolution of military discipline. In fact, in a commander severity is much more necessary than softness, as one gathers from Caesar, who, although he was good-natured and ready to pardon in all other things, was always severe in war. He was not therefore hated by the troops but held in an unbounded affection. So we daily see that those who try to gain the affection and favor of soldiers by giving them too great liberty are in the long run hated and blamed by them and those who are rigorous with them to make them keep good order are loved, revered, and highly praised.

Therefore all leaders must maintain justice and order* in war and rigorously punish transgressors according to the exigencies of the situation.

This rigor must even be preserved in the case of individuals or groups and not only when it is a question of an army or a great force. In this case it is sometimes necessary to dissimulate for a while in order to avoid a greater evil. After the danger is over, however, the leader should try by all means to carry through the punishment or so set about doing it that all will know that such derogation of the authority of the prince or of the commander and such scandal to the commonwealth will not be borne with. Thus no bad consequences will follow therefrom and people will be kept in awe for the future.

CHAPTER XI
*Of the Treatment That the Commander Must Accord to the Soldiers to Keep Them in Good Obedience and Order**

By protecting their rights and not plundering them, but rather treating them liberally according to individual merit when he can reasonably do so, the commander should also to the best of his ability deprive the soldiers of all occasion to disobey him and engage in mutiny. Especially he must not defraud them of their pay in any manner, nor delay its disbursement, but if there is a delay show himself displeased by it and be very diligent to speed it up. Moreover he should treat them with every courtesy of word and deed in his power. If there is a lack of provisions or other necessities in the army he must console and comfort the soldiers by every means he can and show in fact that he is suffering with them in everything. He must let the army know that his heart is completely with them and that he is displeased by all the evils and troubles that they, both the small and the great among them, suffer, and yet always preserve his authority and majesty, especially toward the disobedient.

He should also sustain and have as friends the captains who command companies and some of the chief soldiers, standing in highest credit and authority with the others. He should have some special companies of whom he expects special service, and favor them in whatever way he can, buoying them up with praise, showing special confidence in them, yet always doing this in such a way that the others will rather desire to surpass them through good service than envy the favors that the leader shows them. He will achieve this if his favor is founded on good reason and the merits of those whom he favors, as was the case with Caesar with respect to the tenth legion.[14] If this course is followed there will scarcely ever be any mutiny or disobedience in the army; or if any should take place it will be easily appeased by maintaining the authority of the commander and military discipline.

CHAPTER XII
Of the Way of Life That Soldiers Ought to Live

The second point of discipline lies in the way the soldiers live among themselves. This should be upright, peaceful, and simple. Honor is necessary both to avoid offending God and for the good of the commonwealth. For this reason the leader should order that the name of God and the saints be not blasphemed in his army, sharply punishing those who do it, protect the churches and churchmen from all violence, as well as orphans, widows, and other poverty-stricken folk, and forbid the rape of women and all other things displeasing to God and likely to arouse His wrath. By such offenses and even lesser ones great evils have happened to many armies, as one reads in the Bible and in ecclesiastical and profane histories as well. For the same reason the leader should do his best to prevent common women of ill fame from following his army, as Scipio Africanus did in Spain.[15] If he cannot do this entirely, but to avoid greater difficulties has to tolerate it—just as the church tolerates places of public prostitution in cities, although it does not permit or approve the

14. Caesar *The Gallic Wars* 1. 40.
15. Livy 57.

sin—at least he should prohibit and limit an overgreat number of them and, for the rest, detest lechery and show by word and deed that he disesteems those who make a practice of it and esteems those who live decently and in fear of God. This is more essential for military men than any others, as they are most of the time in danger of their lives. For this reason they should especially put and keep themselves in a state of grace, a thing that is little cared for in France, particularly among the infantry, who ordinarily are so ill conditioned in everything, and especially in respect to blaspheming the name of God, the Virgin Mary and the saints, that they seem not to be reputed men of stout heart unless they do it. Therefore it is not surprising that they scarcely do anything of note. The soldiers also ought to live in peace and the commander avail himself of every means to prevent brawls from breaking out among them, and, if one should occur, immediately to appease it. For brawls may occasion much trouble, as has often happened, especially when there are people of divers nations in the army. To achieve this end, besides what has been said above in discussing obedience, it is very useful to quarter the troops of the various nations as far apart as possible and to take care that in quarters, at the distribution of rations, and in pillaging they have no occasion to mix with each other, and for the rest to bring it about that the captains and their chief subordinates understand and are on good terms with each other.

Thirdly, the soldiers' life should be simple. They should be not too solicitous for their own ease or live too softly either with respect to eating and drinking or with respect to their garb and other luxuries of their person. In this respect it seems that military discipline has been almost entirely lost in most of Europe, but especially in France, because soldiers of all kinds are today accustomed to live as much at their ease in camp as regards food and sleeping quarters and all their other conveniences as if they were in good towns or in their homes. Most of them are unwilling to wear their armor except in case of necessity, when they have to fight or fear they may have to do so. If they wear it, it is only the lesser part, the rest being borne by their pack horse or their valets. From this softness many evils rise.

The first is that, living in this way, they lose vigor and become effeminate, as happened to Hannibal and his men sojourning in luxury at Capua and other places of the Campagna.[16]

In the second place, they must have a remarkable quantity of all kinds of rations to satisfy them, and lacking these they cannot bear up long, even though they have the necessities of life, if not exquisite dainties. Thus some stir mutinies among their companions, and others because of the change in the manner of their life become ill and die, which would not have happened if they had become accustomed to a sober and military life.

Thirdly, the many men and beasts, useless in war but necessary to carry rations and baggage, bring about high prices and famine in the army. They make for disorder because they get in the way of the fighting troops, often holding up the whole army, and besides they always need a large unit to guard them when battle is at hand or in prospect. Sometimes the cavalrymen (who fear to lose their pack animals) break ranks to save them; or the infantry of the same force, instead of fighting, make an attack on the baggage of their own cavalry, whence much trouble has come in our time.

Fourthly, the cost of such superfluous rations, garb, and baggage for their comfort is so great that the soldiers cannot possibly live off their pay.

16. Ibid., 23. 18. 10–16.

CHAPTER XIII

Concerning the Order and Police* Which the Military Ought to Hold to with Respect to the Subjects and Friends of the Prince

Thus arises great disorder which ought to be cut down and reduced to good order. This is the third point about discipline. When the soldiers do not get enough pay to cover their expenses, they rob and ransom the subjects and friends of the prince, for which they are hated everywhere, and especially in lands and lordships newly conquered, so that if any crises comes upon them they fear rather the men on their side than the enemy. For this reason they are constrained to abandon towns and defensible places, which they would not do if they lived in such a way with the people of the country that they could trust them, as experience has shown several times in our day.[17] This is lesson enough that care should be taken in the future so that those who want French domination because of bad treatment at the hands of others do not cease to want it, because they think it cannot be reformed. If it is understood that order* will be upheld and men forced to keep it, there will scarcely be a foreign nation, especially among those subject to mutations, which will not desire the French rather than any other nation in the world. But this order* must be instituted in such a way and so promptly in the realm that the reform may be noticed and the rumor of it set abroad.

17. Including Seyssel's own Milanese experience.

FOURTH PART

Relations with Neighboring Lands, Princes, and Foreign Peoples

Enough has been said concerning this subject of the principles* and order to be held to with respect to the armed forces within the realm and outside it in time of war. It remains to speak of the principles* and conduct that the sovereign of France ought to follow externally with his neighbors, other princes, and foreign nations in times both of peace and of war for the security of this realm.[1] This will be the most difficult part of the treatise and in my opinion the most useful, because with respect to the polity* and armed force in domestic affairs adequate means to maintain them are known to many notable persons, but it is a far greater problem to know how to live and conduct oneself with the foreign nations surrounding this realm on all sides: on the east Italy, Savoy, and the Swiss, on the west England, Brabant, Holland, and Lower Germany, on the south Spain, and on the north Germany. It is much easier to know how to live with

1. Cf. Louis XII's letters concerning the *grand conseil*, 13 July 1498 (Isambert, vol. 11, no. 6), which are seminal for the beginnings of modern French diplomacy. In this part Seyssel shifts conspicuously from classical topics to modern experience, and to this subject there is still no better introduction than Willy Andreas, *Staatskunst und Diplomatie der Venetianer* (Leipzig, 1943); there is more general discussion in various treatments of Machiavelli's theory and practice and more formally in M. de Maulde-la-Clavière, *La Diplomatie au temps de Machiavel* (Paris, 1892–93), esp. 1:91ff.

subjects that one knows and can command than with others whom one does not know, at least not well enough, and also cannot command. Nevertheless, on such knowledge depends in great measure the peace, preservation, prosperity, and increase of every monarchy and all states. If the practice here is hard, the theory, involving the enunciation of specific laws and doctrine as to how to manage relations with neighbors and foreigners, is harder, because the rules vary according as the princes, habits, desires, and affairs of the foreigners change and vary. For some with whom it was formerly good to live in peace and friendship and treat as good neighbors and friends today must be held as enemies and guarded against as bad neighbors. On the other hand, those who have been guarded against as enemies may have to be favored and aided as friends. For this reason, and also because it would be most unpleasant to go into particulars on this matter, I will speak of it only in general terms in such a way that what is to be done in particular cases can be easily understood.

CHAPTER II
How the Princes Ought to Keep the Peace and in What Cases It Is Permissible to Make War

First I will lay it down as a maxim that if they can hope for a sound, true, and complete peace all good princes and others ruling a state or lordship ought to love and seek peace with all neighbors and foreigners except those who, like the infidels, are enemies by nature or diversity of law. Nor should war be declared on any out of desire to dominate for the sake of earthly glory or other disordered passion, but only to recover one's own which has been unduly seized, if it cannot be got back by any other means, or to gain reparations for harm unjustly inflicted on the prince or his subjects, for which compensation cannot be had by friendly means, or finally, to aid and defend neighbors, allies, relatives, and friends, whom others seek unjustly and violently to attack. In these instances it is permissible to declare war according to divine and human law.[2] One may do so with even better cause for the defense of oneself or one's lands and subjects. Such action in this instance is not only permissible but necessary, having always special consideration for the appropriate circumstances, concerning which I do not wish to speak at present, as it is beyond my purpose and would require a special treatise.

CHAPTER III
Of the Precautions and Means That the Prince Should Use to Protect Himself from Neighbors of Whom He Is Suspicious

Because men are ordinarily by their nature corrupt, ambitious, and greedy for domination, especially princes and other rulers of great states, so that one cannot put faith or trust in them, all princes in charge of governing states living in peace with their neighbors must always keep an eye on their affairs and hold themselves ready so that neighboring states may not have the power to do them wrong. In this matter they must make preparations and provide means according to the character and quality of persons, times, and places. For if some neighboring state has power enough in men and wealth to offend and has a feud or ancient ill will against the king and the realm, it is always more necessary to prepare against him than against another who has not the power or the ill will, or who has only one of them. Similarly, if the prince or rulers of a neighboring state are treacherous, mali-

2. In general, Frederick Russell, *The Just War in the Middle Ages* (Cambridge, 1975), and Robert P. Adams, *The Better Part of Valor: More, Erasmus, Colet and Vives on Humanism, War and Peace* (Seattle, 1962).

cious, vicious, and covetous, they must be handled more wisely and circumspectly than if they were men of good faith or little courage or without the adroitness or valor to attack.

To go a little more deeply into this matter, with respect to the former sort, of whom one must be most careful, in times of peace relations with them should be such that they have no reasonable cause to feel aggrieved or to start a war or a crisis. Moreover, as much friendliness to and confidence in them should be displayed and as much desire for their good and prosperity as they show on their side. Nevertheless, knowing their dissimulation and that they would attack if they had the power and the opportunity, every means should be taken within the bounds of honesty and reason to guard against them. This can be done by divers means in accord with God and reason, always preserving the rule of charity. Concerning these means I will only speak of the ones which I recall at the moment. From these the others may be understood, at least by men who have ample knowledge of such matters of state, particularly those of France.

The first means is never to permit such neighbors, whatever friendship they display towards you, to do anything in your lands by means of which they can strengthen themselves against you at the moment or in the future. They should not be allowed to enter, pass through, or sojourn in your lands with a great force under arms, to import from it equipment or food in extraordinary amounts, to have dealings with those who have charge of your strongholds, towns, and fortresses, especially important ones on the frontier, except as necessary for the maintenance of friendship, depending on the quality of the persons involved.

The second is always to keep frontier strongholds well provisioned and protected so that they cannot be surprised, since relaxing sometimes gives men, especially untrustworthy ones, occasion to do what otherwise one would not have expected.

Thirdly, the king should support his own friends and servants from whom he can get aid against troublemakers and never abandon or disregard such allies in his treaties, still less allow them to be ruined and enfeebled by his reconciled enemies, however good a face the latter may put on it or whatever the occasion may be. For if he permits this, besides taking away from such friends the power to serve him when needed, he also takes from them the will and gives them occasion to take sides with the enemy, since they see that they are abandoned when the king thinks he has no further need of them. Thus the appetite of the enemy is whetted to make trouble when he sees the chance. Moreover, to win over an ally from another is a double advantage. First, in one blow the enemy is enfeebled and oneself strengthened. Second, when an ally of one side is abandoned and thus constrained to join the other, the remaining allies of that side lose their courage, and, though not under the same necessity, do the same thing. For the same reasons the prince must not permit the oppression of his own subjects living near the frontier, especially if the neighboring ruler is hostile. On the contrary, in order to give them heart always to be faithful and to sacrifice everything to the cause of their prince, he must on every occasion maintain their quarrels and protect them by all the means he can reasonably deploy.

The fourth means is to prevent such suspect neighbors from becoming so great and strong in friends, allies, riches, and lands that they can inflict harm. To do this is permissible in good conscience to him who can reasonably and legitimately fear that such neighbors, growing in strength, will undertake to do him harm. Thus did St. Paul, who raised a schism among the Jews when he saw that they conspired to harm him contrary to right.[3] From this example any good prince is allowed in such instances by all good and covert

3. Acts 23:1–10.

means to stir up and maintain dissensions among those whose agreement he knows would wrongfully harm him and his subjects, and even between princes and their subjects, provided always that he does so without breaking faith and without procuring treason or misdeeds, for that is never permissible nor honorable. Similarly, while observing the above restrictions it is proper and expedient in such cases to prevent anyone under suspicion from enriching himself with goods or aggrandizing himself with lands, and instead one may use any available reasonable means to put him on the defense and weaken him in goods, power, friends, favor, and everything else with which he would do harm if he could.

Fifth and most important, every wise prince should try, as far as he honorably can, to draw into his service all highly competent counsellors and commanders whom his neighbors, especially the suspect ones, might use against him in great crises. A king of France can do this better than any other prince because his realm has more to offer in the way of great offices and charges to all sorts of people, great, middling, and small, than any other land. These are such that no foreigner, however great, once he has grazed in the French pasture, will ever willingly go away from it, except for very great cause. Those who are drawn to it and treated according to their merits and services come to love the prince and nation so much that they are as good, steadfast, and loyal as the very natives, and abandon the inheritances they have elsewhere for the service of their master. Once their loyalty and worth is established such persons have often received charges, such as the governorships of provinces, towns, and border strongholds, more dangerous and more important than those given to subjects. This realm has received many great services from such foreigners and on the contrary has sometimes refused the services of men who have come back to the fold cheap, and later these have done great harm in the service of an opponent. I do not mean however, that such strangers should be trusted or given charges of great importance at the start or until their virtue, loyalty, and prudence is well known from experience, but that they should be attracted by all honorable means possible.

CHAPTER IV

How the Prince Should Conduct Himself When He Suspects He Will Have War in Some Quarter

All these things are to be taken care of and looked out for when the king is at peace with neighbors of whom he has some fear and whom he cannot reasonably trust altogether. In such cases he should dissimulate with them, not in order to mislead them and deceive them but to obviate their malice and ruses. While doing this he should make preparations always covertly by reasonable and subtle means according to circumstances, without giving his enemies legitimate occasion to feel aggrieved or to break the peace. If he sees that they are preparing for war in such a way that he has good grounds to suspect them, then by remonstrances and all honorable means he should dissuade them from this course, offer to consider any reasonable proposal, and interpose the mediation of friends on both sides, so that first God, then his enemies' subjects and friends and his own, and finally all princes and potentates, especially neighboring ones, may understand that these men of ill will are doing a great wrong, to the great regret of the king. By this means he places God and the world on his side, wins the heart of his subjects and friends to help him gladly and willingly to the best of their power, and weakens and chills the heart of the hostile party. Nevertheless, in this case, without employing any dissimulation he must prepare and strengthen himself in all ways to avoid being surprised, always be ready to defend himself, and even to take the offensive if necessary, for he has no better way to keep the peace than to show himself strong and without fear of the enemy. On the other hand, nothing so incites all men of ill will to war than to see their enemy weak and terrified. Therefore, it is never useful nor honorable, especially for a great prince, to humiliate himself before his enemy, especially before one from whom he has received insults and base treatment, nor to go and seek peace from him except in case of extreme necessity. Above all he must not seek peace from a covetous, ambitious, proud populace or prince, for this only doubles their boldness and takes heart from the supporters of one who shows himself so timorous. He who begs in this manner can never hope to have a reasonable peace. In this matter he should follow the examples of the Athenians in the Persian war and of the Romans in all their great affairs, especially against Hannibal, for they showed such valor and constancy, however hard pressed they were, as never to seek peace with their enemies nor to accept it on dishonorable terms. Even more should a great and noble prince show this virtue.[4]

Besides preparing the armed force to resist a menacing enemy, the prince must employ all devices he can think of to injure him without waiting for the war to start; for just as it is timidity to fear the enemy too much, it is temerity not to esteem him at all, and stupidity not to take measures in time. It is a most disgusting thing for a prince to say when things go contrary to his expectation, "I would not have attempted it," if the outcome could have been foreseen.

Beyond doubt, in war and everywhere else, especially in matters of state, foresighted schemes undertaken and executed with good advice are as useful as mere force, or more so, especially when carried out wisely. By such shrewd

4. Herodotus *The Persian Wars* bks. 6–9; Polybius 9. 5–9; and Livy 12. 42–61.

strokes of diplomacy war can be averted or diverted elsewhere, even on him who sought to make it. Indeed the most effective course available to a prince to keep his state in peace and prosperity is to try by every means available to make war recoil on those disposed to wage it against him, or in every possible way to occupy and divert them elsewhere. For besides the dangers of losing one's land by the hazards of war, great ills follow in the wake of war in the areas of combat, wherein the defender is continually subject to trouble, whereas the assailant, who does not fear being attacked, can rarely lose, and may gain greatly.

For these reasons and others Scipio Africanus, the destroyer of Carthage, persuaded the Romans, when their state was endangered by the great victories of Hannibal in Italy, to go and wage war against the Carthaginians in Africa, whence ensued the salvation and establishment of the Roman Empire and the destruction of the Carthaginian. Soon after, Hannibal gave the same counsel to King Antiochus, who was at war with the Romans, and it went ill with the latter because he did not believe it.[5]

Without offering ancient examples, there has been enough experience of this in our time to teach the error of the opinion that it would be less prejudicial to sustain war in some corner of the kingdom for ten years, provided there was no great loss (thereby retaining the money which would go out of the realm and not come back into it), than to wage war for one year abroad. The entire realm has been more hurt and damaged during the year it sustained a war in one of its extremities, though losing nothing very important, than in ten years of war in Italy.[6] I am indeed of the opinion that it would be better to acquire one town on the borders of the realm, if this could be done justly and without precipitating a

5. Polybius 13. 1–10; 14. 1–19; 21. 6–48.
6. E.g., the English invasion of 1513, culminating in the "battle of the spurs" and the capture of Thérouanne.

greater war, than six that are far away. Of this I will speak later.

To finish the matter we were speaking of, I say that the main means of living in good repute and peace with all foreign neighbors and keeping them from undertaking war against the realm is to manage the affairs of the state in good order, to be provided and prepared to resist all sudden onslaughts, to be able to strengthen oneself to resist a well-prepared major effort, to maintain one's friends at all times so that one can use them in case of need, and always to have schemes and means to divert the war elsewhere or to prevent it and keep busy those who want to wage it.

CHAPTER V

How It Would Be Expedient to Maintain a Navy

Although the kingdom of France is more ready to resist all attacks than any other state whatever because of the union and affection of the subjects in devotion and obedience to the sovereign, because of the ease of raising money, and because of the maintenance of a regular cavalry, nevertheless another thing would be very useful for its defense as well as for its reputation, that is, to be powerful at sea, since this sea surrounds France on two sides. By this means not only would the maritime regions, which are great, powerful, and good lands, be held securely at all times, but all neighboring countries that border the ocean would be kept in fear, whereby the intercourse of trade would be easier, freer, and more secure for the French than it is now. This would result in great profit to the whole realm. If the king should have war with any of these neighbors, being the more powerful he would prevent their taking to the sea and constrain them to be in armed readiness everywhere in their own land where it could be attacked from the sea. Thus he would put them to a double expense and make them fear for their land; and they would be afraid to attack the maritime regions of this realm by sea, lest they be surprised by the French navy.

Moreover, because of the ability to take to sea, a single army adequately equipped could serve easily against several distant lands far apart, as a land-bound army could not do. Of this, besides the experience in recent times of strong maritime cities such as Venice and Genoa, there are examples in ancient histories that peoples strong at sea have done greater things and more rapidly than those with only land armies. This is true of the Athenians, the Carthaginians, and even the Romans, who made no great conquests until they were powerful at sea. Above all other examples the most clear-cut is that of the war which Pompey waged against the pirates, for in sixty days he purged the whole sea and rendered it navigable and so gave security to all the cities and provinces of the Roman Empire on the sea, or near it, which had all been pillaged right up to the city of Rome, and none dared to go to sea except by grace of the pirates.[7] Even with several armies and much time this feat of Pompey's could not have been achieved by land.

The advantages of sea power for doing great things in a short time are thus indicated by Pompey's achievement and also that of the pirates earlier. They were men of small substance, but nevertheless, by means of sea power, in a short time they put the Roman Empire and the city of Rome itself in such fear and necessity as to leave them at loss for a remedy. The trouble would have been even more extensive had it not been for the great valor and authority of Pompey. Because the maintenance of warships would be very costly, however, and a great expense to the king and the commonwealth, and a great increase of charges on the people, I realize that it would be difficult to work out. Nevertheless, if

7. Cicero *Pro Lege Manilia*, pp. 40–48, and Plutarch's life of Pompey.

there were fear and likelihood of naval war the outlay would have to be made, as has been seen in years past; and if it had been made adequately and in time, much other damage and loss would have been prevented, and perils averted.[8]

Of course if war did not threaten our shores no outlay would be necessary and one that heavily burdened the people would be inexpedient, but it seems to me that as the regular cavalry maintained in peace as well as in wartime is the real security of the realm and the terror of neighboring states, so regular warships maintained in such number as the realm could support without being overburdened and the inexpensive regular infantry I suggested above could perpetually secure the kingdom of France in all quarters, and in a little while the kingdom would attain to such greatness and reputation that it would give law to all others. Besides the glory that the king who did this would acquire thereby and the reputation he would confer on the whole French nation, much profit would accrue to both from it: to the prince increase in possessions which he could conquer easily and hold and to the inhabitants of the realm increase in wealth because of the trade that they would carry on by sea in complete safety. For because of this security many Frenchmen would engage in trade who do not dare to do so now for fear of its perils. The extraordinary expenditures necessary anyhow in case of a crisis would be avoided both because no one would dare to attack the realm and because if anyone did, our power would be so great and ready that it would crush the assailant before he could carry out his assault. And if several joined together some would always be given so much to do that they could not, indeed would not have the means to, aid the others.

Therefore I say that although to the people and to those who do not consider consequences this charge seems bur-

8. Referring again to the war with England, 1513–14.

densome at first sight, nevertheless when afterward they become aware of the general wealth and profit resulting therefrom to the king and the whole kingdom the charge would
seem light. In this matter care would have to be taken that
the people who get the most profit from the navy, such as
those who live in maritime regions and carry on maritime
trade, bear the greater part of the expense, and also that the
cost, especially that laid on the people, be limited as much as
possible considering the situation and the time. Moreover, it
is most essential to see to it that the maritime provinces are
always equipped with many good ships which are not a
charge on the king or the commonwealth. In case of necessity
these can be used greatly to aid the regular navy. With trade
secure for the French into all realms many men, seeing the
great profit that other nations make on the sea, would apply
themselves to it; they would have built and equipped for
trade ships which would afterwards be useful in war if occasion arose.[9] All subjects of princes and potentates powerful
at sea do this, as experience tells us. Because the development of sea power could not take place quickly, the king and
the men in charge of the commonwealth under him should
consult with people who understand such matters on the
means for directing and forwarding it.

Although I could propose some methods, yet because it is
not my profession and I do not know enough about it, I will
only say further on the subject that if the king wants to consider it he can receive plenty of good proposals besides the
excellent ones already advanced. As a matter of common
knowledge I will mention one scheme used by the neighbors
of this kingdom to the prejudice of its subjects, of which the
king could always avail himself more easily than any of his
neighbors without doing them wrong and without any

9. Cf. Charles de la Roncière, *Histoire de la marine française* (Paris, 1923),
3:81–128.

danger of war or dispute because of it. It is, not to permit foreign ships to load provisions or other French merchandise for export. This kingdom is so plentiful in goods that it can get along better without all its neighbors than they can without it, and therefore its king can more readily lay down the law about what is carried out of this realm than others can with respect to what is exported from theirs. And unless there be some agreement against it, this would not give them any grounds for grievance since it would not be doing anything to them which they on their side do not do. For such agreements little regard is usually shown, in which case means could be found to remedy the situation wholly or partly. The only problem involved in this or other matters mentioned above is to pay heed to them and get sensible advice. To the French monarchy many things are easy that are impossible to others, and it is enough for me to have put the proposal forward to give men occasion to consider it, because if that happens plenty of knowledgeable and experienced men will be found better able than I to propose ways and means.

FIFTH PART
The Method of Conquering States and Holding Them

In this last part of my treatise I will touch on a point as
needful for the conservation and increase of this monarchy as
any of the others of which I have spoken: the means and
methods necessary to conquer states and lands separate and
distant from the realm, and then what must be done to hold
and preserve them. Above we have mainly touched on what
is expedient for the maintenance and preservation of the
realm and its augmentation in riches and repute; but the
king, well advised, for good reason, and with a good and just
grievance, may at some future time be moved or constrained
to make some conquests outside his realm. In the past and
recently such conquests have proved very expensive both in
good and honorable men and in money, and although well
based have not lasted long; and taking all things together the
kingdom has suffered as much or more shame and harm in
losing them than it has acquired honor and profit from win-
ning them.[1] Therefore, if the question rises of recovering
what has been lost or of making new conquests, it seems
very necessary to take thought and understand the faults that

1. A significant change of mind since Seyssel's celebration of the victory
over the Venetians four years before, though of course his view had no effect
on the young Francis I, on the verge of invading Milan and enjoying a bril-
liant victory at Marignano (13–14 Sept. 1515).

have been committed in the past in order to obviate them in the future, always however, without particularizing or blaming anyone, but only speaking in general terms, as we have done previously.

CHAPTER II
Things to Be Taken into Consideration and Provided for Before Engaging in Any Military Undertaking

Before they engage in such enterprise all princes and other rulers of states must first of all gravely consult on it, and have debated all the grounds on which they claim the lands that they wish to recover or conquer in order to know if those grounds are just and can be maintained before God and the world. If they do otherwise God, Whose justice and truth is infallible, will not aid them; and if for a while He allows the people they seek to overrun to be deprived of their heritage because of their sins, nevertheless the end of the matter is never good. If He does not impose punishment in this world on men who occupy the inheritance of others against reason and conscience, they cannot escape it in the other, and when they die it profits them little to have conquered the whole world but lost their own soul and received eternal damnation, as Our Savior says in the Gospel.[2]

After the king has resolved this first and main question, secondly he must consider the means available to execute the enterprise and the obstacles that may be involved. He must decide whether the enterprise is feasible, as far as he can understand from the opinion of wise and expert men, and if there are evident means to execute it without too much risk, or if the danger is greater than the hope of success. Where it is a matter of the defense of the state or of avoiding some great damage, he may at times have to take risks so long as

2. Mark 8:36.

there is some hope that chance will be favorable. If, however, it is a question of conquest freely undertaken without constraint and only in hope of profit, he must be more cautious and avoid risks where the likelihood of success in the attempt is slight, for without risk scarcely any exploit of war is possible. In such instances it is better to delay ten years than to act one day too soon. If, however, the enterprise must be undertaken for some other end than profit, for example, for honor, and no delay is possible without hurt to honor, then the king must take his chances, just as he must for the defense of what he holds or to avoid a great loss, because a noble prince must esteem loss of honor worse than loss of riches. He must do so likewise if delay in conquest would bring irreparable harm to his own land—if through delay, for example, the state in question would be in danger of falling in the hands of his enemy who thereby could afterwards do great harm to his kingdom.

All these considerations are matters of practice and require experience more than instruction. For instance the nature, condition, and skill of the king's own people, of friends from whom aid and favor may be expected, and of the enemy and his partisans should be known, as well as the outlay necessary, whether it would be available in time, what the enemy on his side can do, the character of the land to be conquered, the roads and passes of entry and egress, and all other such matters that men experienced in war know most about. Above all the king must not succumb to schemes without solid foundation, nor to the persuasions of men hotheaded or ignorant of such matters, nor to his own appetite and desire, but always take the gloomiest view of what is likely to happen, depending on the present state of affairs or on what seems likely in the future.[3]

3. Referring perhaps to Charles VIII's invasion of Italy in 1494, on which he read Philippe de Commynes, *Mémoires*, bk. 7, and perhaps reflecting anxiety about the young Francis I.

After everything has been considered and debated, if good advice suggests that the king can undertake the enterprise and come out on top, he must in the third place consider whether he has the means to hold and preserve the land he seeks to conquer and what its revenue is. For if it is quite clear that if it cannot be kept it would be manifest folly to seek to conquer it, only to lose the cost, the time, and one's honor. In this case he must consider whether he has the means to remove the obstacle likely to cause the loss of the land, once it has been conquered. If so, the means must be used before undertaking the enterprise or while undertaking it, whichever is easier; if not, it is better to let the enterprise go and consider something else more honorable and profitable. The same is true if to make a conquest would involve a greater outlay than can be regained from it, and if the land costs more to keep than any profit it could possibly bring. For we read that the Romans and others for this very reason refused lands which wanted to surrender to them willingly. It was not without cause that I said "If the outlay should be greater than *any* profit," for the cost may surpass the revenue and yet the importance of the place be so great for the security of other states, or for its convenience as a passage, or for some other such reasons, that one must give greater consideration to them than to the outlay involved, and balance them against one another.

Likewise when for a while the outlay to conquer and hold a country or town would be excessive, but there is reasonable hope that in a short time it will decrease and the revenue increase, one must not hesitate at this outlay; anyone who did not look at things this way would scarcely undertake a conquest at all, since at the outset the outlay is always greater than the profit. To conclude briefly, even though the enterprise would be easy enough, its utility and necessity must be considered with respect both to the present time and the future, both with respect to honor and profit, just as one does who wants to buy an office or benefice which he cannot gain without trouble and expense, and which he is not sure of obtaining, or if he obtains it, of holding it peacefully.

CHAPTER III
Things That Are Necessary for Waging War

After all this thought has been expended and the enterprise resolved on, it must be executed speedily and as soon as possible after all preparations have been made, for delay gives time and leisure to the enemy to strengthen himself and make ready his defense by force and craft. Moreover, on the side of him who undertakes the enterprise, once the matter becomes known, hearts become cool, the expense increases, and the opportunity is lost with the passage of time, from which some obstacle can rise to block the whole operation. Yet the operation must not be so sped up that the necessary equipment is lacking.

Secondly, the king must put his whole mind to its execution and have provisions so prepared to meet all emergencies that there will be no deficiency or delay in any single item. To this end there must be men expert, faithful, diligent, and in adequate number so that charges can be distributed and commissions issued severally to various persons who will not put obstacles in each other's way. Above all there must be a commander of the kind and with the power and authority described above. Moreover, if the prince is not present in the theater of operations he must depute a number of the chief councillors at his side to do nothing but consider and deal with the war; and he himself must consult with them if he has to make some answer or provision in the matter, so that everything may be done promptly. These two things are most essential in all matters especially in war.

Thirdly, he must avail himself of every means to harm his

enemy, whether by craft or by force, and in so doing not undervalue anything great or small to strengthen his enterprise or to deprive his enemy of friends and favor. Moreover, he must spare nothing that he can possibly supply to shorten the enterprise, and rather make a double outlay to execute it promptly than to save by means of delay, for delay quadruples the expense, not to mention the dangers and the risks.

In waging war the French especially must set to work as fast as they can, for they are much better at the outset and the first thrust than when because of long delay they have to act in cool blood.[4] For the same reason, what can be had without risk for money or by craft should be taken quickly without waiting to get it afterwards by force. This requires no further discussion because it is the concern of those who have charge of such undertakings. Nevertheless, although I know that the military chiefs understand them very well, I wanted to mention these three points because in our time, within living memory, many errors with respect to them have been committed, whence many calamities have followed.

CHAPTER IV
Concerning the Means to Keep States and Lordships Newly Recovered or Conquered

There remains only the second point of this section, that is how to keep such newly conquered lands for a long time. And although by experience, observation, and reading the treatises and histories mentioned above everything to be said on this score can be easily understood, nevertheless, following the methods that I have held to thus far in this treatise, I will reduce to a few words the points that seem

4. Cf. Machiavelli, *Discourses* 3. 36, and Livy 10. 28. 4; but of course Seyssel could draw on his own Milanese experiences.

fundamental to me at the present time and about which there has been most error recently. Thus the reasons why the French lost the lands that they have conquered may be understood and judged.

To cut the matter short, it must be assumed that in these affairs two things are necessary, armed force and political organization.* The first is necessary at the outset, for despite the obedience that a conqueror finds in the beginning he must not relax his armed power until the situation is stable, but must follow up the victory to put an end to the war so that if possible he will not have to resort to it again. Once this is done—a good order instituted in all necessary matters with respect to justice and political organization,* and the affairs of the state made secure—the army may be disbanded and withdrawn to avoid the burden it places on the conquered land involved. For a while, however, until by long experience one is very sure of the good will of the subjects and the complete security of the state with respect to its neighbors, a considerable number of soldiers must be kept there to defend it, to prevent all sudden crises, and to enforce obedience to the officers of justice, political organization,* and finance. The arrangements concerning justice and police,* however, are much more essential because they must last permanently, and it is by them that the estate of the soldiers and the armed force is regulated.

CHAPTER V
Of Matters Concerning the Armed Force in General

However, I will commence with the armed force without repeating what I said above, when speaking of the preservation of the realm and of military discipline, all of which applies in this case. But there are certain things the king must do to hold a land newly conquered that he need not do to hold his ancient heritage. To these every conqueror must give close attention. In the first place he must consider the most obvious and predictable dangers by which he may lose the newly conquered state and, according as they are great or small, make the necessary preparations. Among other things he must consider first whether the prince who lost the state or any member of his house is alive and able to raise opposition;[5] secondly, whether the people generally or any particular factions are inclined to that house, and whether it is the weaker or the stronger faction; thirdly, whether the neighboring princes or states are friendly, hostile, or neutral; fourthly, whether the land is well supplied with routes, abundant provisions, and other things to make it defendable, or whether it is poorly supplied; fifthly, whether it is far from or near to the land of the conqueror, whence aid can come. Taking all these things into consideration, if the security of the land is such that no great garrison is needed, the smallest possible one should be left both to avoid the cost to and oppression of the land and its subjects and because soldiers naturally want the fights and wars that are their livelihood. Therefore they may easily start some brawl with a neighboring land which would be the beginning of a great war. Moreover, however good the order* they maintain as regards pay, they always do many things unpleasant to the inhabitants of the land, especially with respect to women and quarters. In fact, they are company not much wanted except in case of necessity. So, for all of the reasons that we have spoken of before, if a great force must be kept in the place, the manner of doing so must be carefully considered. For if the conquered land is suspect and well populated with warlike people, or if the people there are not warlike and there are powerful enemies near by, wholly foreign soldiers must be left behind. This is very expensive and a source of many evils because those who have gathered good booty or

5. Cf. Machiavelli, *The Prince*, chap. 6.

otherwise profited always want to take it home; and if those
who do not get a chance to are to be kept in good order*—
and they must be, as I will show later—they can scarcely
maintain themselves on their wages and so are forced to
abandon the country. Those who out of a sense of honor do
not do so at least wish for an honorable excuse to withdraw
and therefore care little whether the land is lost so long as
they are saved. Besides, knowing that the soldiers care little
for them and find their company more an annoyance and a
nuisance than a profit and a pleasure, the people of the land
desire to be free of them and readily give their support to
anyone who wants to chase them out, although the change
might be for the worse, because, blinded by hate and passion, they fail to realize this until after the act. When all this
concurs with ill will on the part of both the inhabitants and
the soldiers, it is impossible or very difficult to hold a country over the long run.

CHAPTER VI
*Of the Measures That Must Be Taken When the People of a
Newly Conquered Land Cannot Be Trusted*

If only a garrison kept there to coerce the inhabitants could
secure the land, the prince would be ill advised to undertake
the conquest in order to keep it. If his cause is good he would
do better to make some honorable agreement with its posses-
sor or permit some lord who could help and serve him to
hold it, as did Alexander and the Roman people in divers
places,[6] unless they had to hold the country in their own
hands for the security of some other land so that the profit
exceeded the outlay. In such an instance the best provision
possible must be made against the evils above mentioned.

6. Polybius 18. 37.

With respect to the soldiers means must be sought to make most of them or their leaders love the land and desire to stay there by giving them a stake that they cannot sell, or marrying them off in the country. In this way they will become acquainted with the inhabitants and desire to live with them. This was what Duke William of Normandy did when he conquered England, for he distributed a great part of it among his men, who thereafter defended it. The Romans and Greeks did the same, founding towns that they called their colonies in suitable places in conquered lands and settling them with their own people to whom they leased houses to dwell in and lands to work. In the course of time these settlers took on the manners and customs of the land, and moreover, since they had decided to live there, dwelt harmoniously with their neighbors, but nevertheless were always ready to take up arms in the cause of their lords, as were other men who came to live in the towns with them, because all were reputed to be of the same nation and enjoyed the same privileges. Other conquerors exiled the inhabitants of the land whose devotion they could not win, and in place of them put their own people or other foreigners whom they brought in from elsewhere.[7] Alexander the Great and his successors did this in several places, but it would be very inhumane and in addition hard to put into practice. The method suggested before would be easier. Moreover, because by such means only a few soldiers could be kept in the conquered country, some other means must be devised with respect to the rest, such as to change them quarterly or annually, as seems most expedient, to pay them higher wages, or confer some other preeminence or advantage on them in their own country, or to give them hope of some profit in war or otherwise if they serve loyally. Those who leave without their leader's permission, or mutiny to go home, or other-

7. 2 Kings 12:4, on the Babylonian captivity.

wise fail to acquit themselves properly must be harshly punished. These are the things, it seems to me, that can be done about soldiers left in conquered lands.

Besides the order* which one makes the soldiers maintain, one must persuade the inhabitants by every possible means to put up with the military docilely, telling them that their money remains in their land, that the garrison will be withdrawn as soon as experience shows that they are good and loyal subjects, that it is there to protect and preserve them against the pillaging of their enemies, and other such things. Above all, good usage from the commander would be helpful, showing that he truly loved the country and its inhabitants and was unwilling to see them oppressed or outraged in their persons, their wives, or their possessions. If the prince himself would remain in the country for a while, it would very much help him win the heart of the people.

Another measure he could try, which all conquerors formerly employed, would be to take the leading men as hostages from the conquered land in such number as he deemed sufficient to keep the rest in fear.[8] He could do this in subtle ways and under the pretext of making use of them in other lands, or raising them in his own realm in order to teach them the language, or under some other such pretense.

CHAPTER VII
Of the Measures to Take When the Confidence of the Inhabitants of the Land Can Be Gained

The course I proposed above would be followed if the king could not by any means feel confidence with respect to the inhabitants of a newly conquered land because of their ill

8. E.g., Livy 37. 45., and Polybius 18. 39; 36. 4.

will or their incompetence in arms. But if they, or enough of them to make use of, can possibly be trusted, the conqueror should take them into his pay, mixing them with the other units of his force, and thus teaching them his people's way of living and waging war, so that they will learn to love his nation. Moreover, he should give some of the leading men office. By this means he wins over not only those who take his wages but also their relatives and friends, gives hope to others, and shows his faith in all of them. They can live on a smaller wage than foreigners and burden the country less; and even if they were not as good as the others, nevertheless time would improve them and they would serve with the others and have no cause to want a political change. For this purpose the better sort must be chosen, especially the gentlemen, the better-born from whom the most service could be expected.

The Romans, the Greeks, and all other conquerors, in olden times made this arrangement, and I do not see how in the long run a prince can keep a distant country where he has to maintain soldiers if he does not employ its inhabitants. This was why the grandfather of the Turk now ruling,[9] after he had conquered Greece and several other realms and provinces from the Christians, realizing that he could not hold them using the men of his own nation, adopted the method of selecting children from the Christians living in the conquered land, which he turned into the soldiery called the janissaries. This tyranny, however, will ultimately bring ruin to that state because these janissaries themselves will weary of the tyrannical and cruel domination of the Turk and divide the state among themselves, especially since they receive no lands or lordships but only wages and office. Therefore it is much more civilized, more reasonable, and easier to follow the course I spoke of.

9. Suleiman's grandfather was Mohamed II.

CHAPTER VIII
How One Must Strengthen, Supply, and Keep Strongholds with
Captains, Soldiers, and Other Things

So much for the armed force with respect to personnel. Tenable strongholds, especially those on the borders and those that can most easily be succored, must be strengthened and supplied with provisions, artillery, ammunition, and whatever is needed to sustain a siege at least for a whole year. The order must be given that such a supply never fails, or if a failure takes place that blame can be fixed. Similarly, the strong places must have able captains and an adequate number of reliable and faithful soldiers who will bear every necessity and extremity so long as there is hope of relief, and who will not consider any treaty with any group of the enemy, except in case of extreme necessity. To be most secure in all this, one must put in these strongholds foreigners without relatives, friends, or goods in the country. For as inhabitants can easily be drawn into schemes, they cannot be trusted entirely until they are very well known and tried, and even of these no great number should be used except in cases of necessity. Above all, the commander must be one who can win love and reverence and must have experience not only in matters of war but also in guarding, supplying, and defending besieged strongholds, for there are those skilled in battle who would be incapable of handling such matters. He must also have great wisdom and discretion, as well as experience to provide remedies and make preparations for the many things that happen in such situations, and especially to give heart and hope to his companions and keep them from mutiny and idle talk. He must also know how to distribute provisions, repair, and make everything necessary in a besieged stronghold. Such commanders must be salaried and provided for in keeping with the importance of the strongholds so that they may have no occasion to behave badly

out of poverty or spite. In addition, they must be known not
to be of the kind too bent on their own profit and schemes,
otherwise even though they are not moved treacherously to
surrender the stronghold, a thing always to be feared in such
men, yet out of greed they will fail to do many essential
things, will never be loved by their comrades, and will be
busy with negotiations to advance themselves outside the
garrison. This is improper and dangerous, for such commanders must not on any condition have any charge or mix
in matters of justice and police* in the town, or do anything
but provide for and keep their strongholds. It is essential that
neither they nor their men ever go far from their places except for very good reason and rarely, and that they have no
important dealings with the inhabitants of town or country,
nor admit them to the stronghold except on business necessary for the stronghold, for thus many evils have ensued before and may again. So much for the armed force.

CHAPTER IX
What Must Be Done about Police* *in Conquered Lands*

With respect to the order of the polity* certainly it is much
more essential to maintain it well in newly conquered countries than in others, and nevertheless the precise opposite is
ordinarily done. Although from what has been said above it
is easy enough to understand what in general must be done
with respect to that order*—that is, maintain sound justice
in the country, force the soldiery to keep order and discipline, and take great pains with such matters having to do
with the political order* of the land as the abundance of
provisions, the movement of commerce, the appeasement of
quarrels, and other such matters—nevertheless I will deal in
detail with some things which to my mind must be understood and executed in detail. Since in this situation all things

likely to be agreeable to all the people or the majority should be done, provided they are not prejudicial to the king and the state, and those that seem generally grievous and unpleasant to the people must be avoided, I will mention some.

First, in the administration of justice no favor must be shown to anyone, but it must be distributed equally and men deputed to the work who understand it and want to do it. Besides satisfying God in so doing the king thereby also usually satisfies the whole people; and even those who want to follow the opposite course for their private ends, if they are refused, will know that they are wrong, and harbor no grudge against the men who do them justice.

Secondly, in matters concerning the mode of life of the subjects which touch the prince's interest little if at all, it is essential to let them live and act as they were accustomed to do of old without constraining them to take on another way of life, at least at the outset, but rather as far as possible, if not as much as the inhabitants themselves wish, to force the foreigners who live among them to conform to their manners and customs.[10] This was one of the means by which Alexander the Great acquired most completely the love and obedience of the lands he conquered, for as he lived according to their customs they realized that he esteemed and loved them and would live and die with them. In the long run, however, and by gentle means depending on the situation, they should be drawn as far as possible to adopt the customs and laws of the prince so that they may forget their own old ways and live in better accord with the prince's other subjects. This policy was pursued by the Romans. If the prince cannot stay long in the conquered land, at least he should show that his sojourn there has pleased him, that he would like to stay there insofar as the opportunity offered, and that he would gladly spend all the rest of his estate and person for the land's

10. Cf. Machiavelli, *The Prince*, chaps. 3–7, and Plutarch's life of Alexander.

defense and preservation. Moreover, he must leave in the conquered land as a lieutenant some good and great person who by reason of his person and dignity will win reverence, providing such a man can be found. In any case, this lieutenant must live honorably and hold court and be surrounded by persons good and notable both in war and in council and have such broad authority that the subjects will honor and obey him as they would the prince himself and have recourse to him for remedies for their grievances, and pardon and grace in matters of minor consequence. Great matters the sovereign should reserve for himself, as has been said above. Likewise, with respect to justice between subjects, the prince should depute a chief with complete authority and a number of others qualified in learning, wisdom, and experience and possessed of knowledge of the laws and customs of the land. Because foreigners cannot attain such knowledge very quickly, a number of the best equipped and most highly reputed men of the country itself must be used. This also will serve to satisfy them. But the chief must be a foreigner, a man highly esteemed, to keep the others along the straight road and decide matters according to reason without fear or favor to anyone. To him the prince and the lieutenant must give every favor and assistance, nor impede in any way whatever the course of justice, but order and enforce whatever is decreed, and for this purpose intervene whenever necessary. If this is done, the subjects will love the prince better and live in great awe of him, whereas if they see that he cares little for them and that his officers and lieutenants are only trying to get out of them what they can without putting in order the things necessary to their preservation, love and awe will be converted into hate and distrust.

Thirdly, the prince and his lieutenants and officers must give honor, welcome, and hospitality to the inhabitants of the land, especially to the leaders—those who have the most authority with the people and who he hopes may be serviceable. To these leaders, their children, relatives, and friends should be given most of the benefices and offices of the land, which they can handle, barring the main offices of state, justice, and finance, which the prince must put in the hands of old and faithful servants chosen as described above. These men should be agreeable to the inhabitants and as conformable as possible to their customs and especially should care more about their conscience and their honor than their profit.

Yet if some of the leaders of the country have done great service and are besides adequate and agreeable to the majority of the people, it is not at all inappropriate to provide them with some of the greatest charges, even the chief one for a while, so long as the prince finds he is being well served. For all nations of reasonable men would rather be governed by those of their own nation, who know their manners, laws, and customs, speak the same language, and have the same way of life as they, than by strangers.

CHAPTER X
How to Govern a Land Riven by Party Strife

There are, however, some nations who will otherwise, and this proceeds from party strife among them, so extreme that those of one faction would rather be ill treated by a foreigner than well governed by one of the opposite faction, however excellent a man he was. In this case the king who has conquered such a country must always appoint as chief a foreigner having the qualities above mentioned or approaching them as nearly as possible, and moreover seek by all means available to extinguish party strife and bring about an accord in devotion to him, if that seems possible. But if he sees that this is impossible he must at least prevent such party strife from displaying itself overtly, especially in mat-

ters of state and the public weal. He must not favor either
party or faction, but only men of substance and probity, of
whatever faction, who demonstrate themselves to be the best
servants and subjects; and he should honor these men and
provide well for them, whichever faction they belong to. This
is the case when he is as much loved and wanted by one
faction as by the other, whatever divisions they have among
themselves in other matters. Yet if he clearly knows by experience or otherwise that one of the factions is propitious and
friendly toward him and the other hostile and opposed, he
should try to strengthen the friendly one by all means at his
disposal, without, however, acting contrary to conscience or
wronging anyone. He can do it by promoting men of the
friendly faction to offices, dignities, charges, and profits, by
giving them estates and lands according to their merit, and
by showing more confidence in them than in the others. He
should make it appear, however, that he does not do so in a
partisan way but only because of the merits and services of
the people he advances, and should do the same for those of
the other faction who turn out sound and loyal. This will
serve to draw the other faction, or some of them, to him.
Moreover, in matters of no importance, and in matters of
private law, however important, he must treat all equally.
But in matters of state involving great profit and authority he
should advance those best affected to the side of the prince.
For it is much better to satisfy the party that will do its best in
support of the prince's cause and to keep the one that cannot
be won over so low it cannot do any harm than to leave the
well-disposed party weak and dissatisfied and strengthen
the one that cannot be brought around. If the prince does the
latter, then both parties, being dissatisfied, may easily come
to an agreement against him. In doing this, however, great
care must be taken to give no one occasion to complain that
he has been wronged, or to realize that the prince and his
chief officers are supporting any party; and in truth he is

supporting none except insofar as is necessary for the security of the state. Moreover, it must be considered whether the opposition party is the stronger or the weaker, for if it is the weaker it can easily be reduced by the means suggested above, or indeed will remain so abased that it can do no harm, and so there is no need to seek to depress it further. If it is the stronger, and experience has shown that it cannot be won over, then an effort must be made to draw off as many as possible of those from whom one can hope any good and to provide for them in such a way that they will have reason to be faithful and others to become so. Moreover, the prince must dissimulate with these last and keep them so low that they can do no harm and that with the aid of the other part he can always suppress them. Especially he must have spies among them, particularly in unquiet times, and if he finds them at fault punish them harshly for it. If the danger is clear-cut, it is permissible and expedient on a reasonable suspicion, even without adequate proof of misdeed on their part, to make sure of them by sending them away, forcing them to give sureties and pledges, placing foreigners in their strongholds, if they have any, and by doing other things, depending on the situation, provided that no loss nor harm be inflicted on them if they be found blameless. All good princes and rulers do this, and it is not contrary to divine law.

[And as to the present prince and monarch of France, there is no doubt that, being endowed with such gifts of nature and grace and having at his age such great and ready power along with the love of his people and especially of his nobility, if he adheres to the above proposals or to what his council advises with respect to the points touched on, he will do greater things more worthy of memory than any king of France has ever done, having God always before him, as he has started out to do. For the events of the day all point in this direction, and God, seeing his good will, will daily more fully aid him and guide him in all his deeds and affairs, so that by his means the recovery of the Holy Land and the empires, realms, countries, and provinces held by the infidel may be brought about, to the honor of God, of our faith and Christian religion, and to the salvation of his soul and the perpetual glory of his name and of the French nation.]

[Here ends *The Monarchy of France*, printed in Paris for Regnault Chauldière, publisher, dwelling on the Rue St. Jacques at the sign of the Wild Man. The printing was completed the 21st day of July the year one thousand five hundred and nineteen. With the privilege of the king our lord as appears on the first leaf of the present book.]

Exordium to the translation of the History *of Justin from Latin to French by Claude de Seyssel, doctor of laws, Councillor and Master of Ordinary Requests of the household of the Most Christian King of France, Louis the twelfth of that name, and addressed to the said king.* [1]

The people and princes of Rome, O Most Christian and most virtuous king, holding the monarchy of the world, which, despite so much striving to perpetuate it and make it eternal nonetheless came to nothing, found no means to accomplish their goal more certain or more reliable than to magnify, enrich, and refine their Latin language, which was quite meagre and rude in the early days of their empire, and afterwards to spread it to the countries, provinces, and peoples they conquered, together with the Roman laws promulgated in the Latin language, of which the conquered lands and people had no previous knowledge.

First of all, in order to augment, exalt, and make illustrious the Latin tongue, they tried to render and translate into their own the Greek language. Greek was at that time the richest, most elegant, most perfect, and the most esteemed of all other languages. In truth, it was the most common language, largely because all the liberal arts, philosophical sys-

1. See introduction, n. 19.

tems, poetry (which is the theology of pagans), and all other things worthy of being known were expressed in that language more amply and more eloquently than in any other.

The Romans devoted themselves so diligently to this task that all these arts and sciences, or at least the majority of them, were translated from Greek into Latin, so that to learn them it was no longer necessary to understand Greek, although knowledge and understanding of that language gave to those studies greater light and intelligibility because it is their true fountain. Thus, through the great talent and labor of many excellent and notable Romans, Latin gradually became as perfect as Greek, as Cicero himself testifies.

That was the reason why other lands and provinces, which have since escaped from obedience to the Roman Empire, have retained the use of its language throughout almost all of Europe—except Greece—or at least in those lands and nations which submit to the Holy See of Rome, because by that means they can communicate with each other through a common language and also have some knowledge of the arts and sciences as well as all the history of the world, both ancient and modern. Thus it is that the greatness of that empire and of the kingdom would not have been preserved if not for the widespread use and authority of the Latin language. Without enumerating all the other ancient conquerors who have brought their language and laws to the lands and people they conquered, one can today point to the example of how Duke William of Normandy, who was a most wise and valiant prince and the first of his people to rule the kingdom of England, wishing to keep it under the domination of his family and nation, gave the English the laws of Normandy, written in that same common language which is used today, as I myself saw when I was recently sent by you [as ambassador] to the late King Henry [VII—Ed.] of good memory.[2]

2. A reference to Seyssel's mission to England in 1506; see introduction, n. 22.

Such things you, too, Sire, have done and do daily with your power. For, in the first place, by means of your great and glorious conquests in Italy there is now no corner of that land where the French language is not understood by most of the people. Thus, where Italians formerly considered Frenchmen barbarians in their customs and language, it is now the case that the two peoples understand each other without the aid of interpreters and the Italians (those who owe obedience to you as well as many others) adapt themselves to the apparel and the way of life of France. And as this continues the two nations will come to have almost the same fashion in everything, just as one sees among the people of Asti and all of Piedmont, who (for having lived so long under the lordship and obedience of you and your predecessors the dukes of Orléans as well as the rulers of Asti, Piedmont, and Savoy who have themselves lived and do now live in a manner quite like the French) are not greatly different from the French in their way of life, understand French quite as well as their own tongue, and use it as often. In addition, the French language is widely published in several other provinces and nations of Europe because of the continuous communication which the princes and peoples of those states now have and have had long since.

Then again, by other means more exquisite and which bring you more praise, you work to enrich and magnify the French language. That is to say, those books and treatises which were originally composed in Greek or Latin you have taken care to have translated into French, just as many of your predecessors among the kings and princes of the blood royal did before you and for which the French nation is much beholden to you. For by this means those who have no knowledge of Latin can learn many good and important things of which they would otherwise have no knowledge, be they in the Holy Scripture, moral philosophy, medicine, or history.

And because I knew, Sire, that this was your noble and

royal wish, and that you take great pleasure from reading or hearing those books so translated, especially histories, which are the true pastime of great princes because they contain not only narratives of events—which is their pleasure and flower—but also lessons and examples for those who see and read them—which is their fruit—I began some years ago to translate Xenophon's history of the travels of Cyrus in Persia[3] even though this is not my proper trade and I had never before undertaken such work, nor was it suitable to my profession or my nationality. Nonetheless, I saw by experience that you took some pleasure in it and that such works are most agreeable to you.

Thus, Sire, this year, when you left the country to lead the war against the Venetians, who had provoked you to it by their pride and disloyalty, I undertook a translation of Justin, who was the epitomizer of Trogus Pompeius (who among all historians is the one whose work is singularly celebrated and recommended because it is universal and treats of all peoples and nations) so that upon your victorious return (which I took as a certainty, as I told you at the time) and when you would grow weary of hearing it spoken of (as one does of all things in this world, especially you who do not like to have your own deeds, however great they may be, praised often in your presence) you would have a new pastime and that those also who might read it after you might judge if yours was not worthy of being placed among the many victories recorded and extolled in that book. For in my judgment, considering the power of your enemies (their rulers, revenues, the members of their council, the commanders, wealth, renown, and ordnance of their military), the great feats they have accomplished, the great powers and lords they have resisted and those they have defeated and

3. The *Anabasis*, presented to Louis XII in 1505.

vanquished, as well as the long duration of their empire and dominion, always with the greatest reputation for power, I consider what you have done against them in so little time, with so little loss and with such great consequence to be as worthy of praise as any of the wars recorded in this or any other history whatever. Moreover, in this campaign of yours you were the initiator, the leader, and the executor; you acted alone and in one day accomplished what seemed difficult to all wise and powerful men.

But as that is not our principal interest just now, I will return to my purpose.

Thus, when I knew that such works as these please you—and even that what I had done as an experiment and more or less to try my hand at it you, either from instinctive courteousness and good nature or to give courage to me and others in such activities, highly praised the undertaking and valued it more than its worth as a translation—then I was determined to persevere in such projects as much not to seem ungrateful to you (who had given me so much honor for the first apprentice piece, as it were) as to satisfy your most noble and worthy wish and desire to have an ever-increasing knowledge of many histories.

Thus, I did not much care if my labors were not agreeable to many others, but only that they might be to your taste for whom (as do many fine cooks) I had and wish to have sole concern. And I count myself happier that my idle musings—however rude they may be—are praised by you alone than if they were extolled by all the world but not by you. For I have not undertaken such a task for any other reason or for any other end than to please you and to do something agreeable for you to whom I consider myself so bound and obligated for many reasons (which I shall leave unsaid just now) that I can never hope—even employing all the time given to me in this life, nor even my body, my soul, my understanding, and all else that I have, which is not all in all a great deal—to render in service one hundredth of the goods and honors that you have given to me.

So I humbly pray, Sire, that you will take a liking to this little gift and that you will not stumble on the mistakes and imperfections of translation which may be in it, but that you will relish the variety of its stories of the birth of nations, cities, and provinces, of the great deeds (which are praised in order to be imitated) and the cowardly ones (which you have always striven to avoid). Moreover, do not be astounded if you find sentences or episodes abridged; for the Justin that we here translate has done this quite deliberately in order to avoid the prolixity of Trogus Pompeius, who wrote so much that he often missed the point.

Similarly, if I imitate the style of the original Latin, do not think that this is by mistake or that I had not been able to express myself in other more commonly used terms, as is the fashion of French histories. But be assured, Sire, that the Latin language of the author is of such great beauty and elegance that as closely as one follows the text so much does it retain its original beauty. This, indeed, is the proper way of making Latin conform with French, just as the Romans made Latin conform with Greek and as it is done to this day in your kingdom with great diligence and care. For both languages have as much or more currency there than in any other place one can speak of; so that (in the near future and to God's great pleasure) your reign will have the honor and glory of having spread the knowledge of those two languages throughout your kingdom and enriching French through its contact with them. That, along with other great and memorable deeds you have done and I hope will yet do, will continue to enhance your name and your memory in this world.

That is something you may justly desire, not principally to the end of attaining glory, which, of all things, you owe and must return to God, but in order to offer an example and lesson to your successors and other princes, who will be considered blessed if they emulate your royal, virtuous, and magnanimous ways. And may God, in his goodness and infinite mercy, give them grace to do greater deeds, if that is possible, and to you, Sire, to persevere and improve so that in His dread and love you will be able to conquer and attain the joy of His eternal kingdom.

Proem by Messire Claude de Seyssel, Councillor and Master of Ordinary Requests of the Household of the Most Christian King of France, Louis the twelfth of that name, to the translation of the history by Appian of Alexandria entitled The Deeds of the Romans.[1]

The Princes and Barons of Persia, O Most Christian and most victorious king, who once, by their good sense and hardihood, murdered the two *mages* who treasonously occupied the kingdom of Persia after the death of Cambyses, having delivered that most powerful and renowned empire from the tyranny of the *mages*, held a great debate over what form of government they would put in place so as to be better and more politically governed. Three opinions predominated among them, as we are told by the great and ancient historian Herodotus in the third book of his *History*.[2]

One among them was of the opinion that they ought to adopt a popular government (what the Greeks called a democracy) in order to avoid tyranny, which most often succeeds a monarchical regime, the rule of a single person, and in which all things are in the power of a single person who exempts himself and is free from all law, is subject to no punishment nor to private reprimand. He who argued for a democracy was of the opinion that affairs of state would be

1. See introduction, n. 21.
2. Herodotus *The Persian Wars* 3. 80–83.

much better conducted if they were handled by a larger number of many sorts of people.

But the second demonstrated with keen reasoning that popular government was even worse than a monarchy, the more so because in a confused multitude of men there can be no good sense, reason, or accord for very long, and thus the democratic regime must surrender to impetuosity, confusion, and discord, which will not so easily arise under a single leader, however bad he may be, as well as all the other inconveniences which follow and which had already been mentioned. The second speaker supported a form of government between the other two which is called "aristocracy," that is, rule of the principal men of greatest wealth. By this means they would avoid both the tyranny of a monarch and the confusion of the multitude.

This argument notwithstanding, the third speaker was of the opinion that monarchy was better, not only than the popular regime, which there seemed no difficulty in demonstrating, but also than the aristocratic regime. As for the latter, no matter how many men are elected to the government, one among them searches out and tries by every means to surpass and excel the others, first in glory and in his reputation among the people, then in authority and the management of affairs, and finally in power and wealth. From this there soon follow, because of emulation and envy, discord, partialities, hatreds, and intrigues; then seditions, mutinies, injuries, and violent acts; and finally murders, expulsions, banishments, and persecutions until there is open civil war. This is a war more cruel, more dangerous, and more to be feared than any which is undertaken against enemies, just as an illness which affects internal organs is more dangerous than one which affects external organs.

This third opinion, just as it was approved and put into effect by the judgment of those sages, has been sustained and found to be accurate by many philosophers and scholars.

It is true that many reasons and arguments could be put forward on one side or the other. And if one could find people such as those who have been described by the many who have spoken on this matter, then each of the reasons would be good and profitable. Nonetheless (given the natural dissension, inevitable ambition, and insatiable covetousness which continually predominates among human beings), when one has carefully considered all the inconveniences which spring up and are born in each kind of state, still it is monarchy which is the most tolerable and most suitable, taken all in all. In addition, one sees that all the great empires which existed before that of the Romans, namely, the Assyrians, the Medes and Persians, and the Greeks in the person of Alexander, were created and governed by a single king. One also sees that most of the world has almost always been governed (and is still governed at present) by kings and monarchs.

Even in the case of Rome, they began the same way. Afterwards, although at certain times power was gained by others, in all their important affairs and extreme dangers they were constrained to give total authority and power for limited times to a single individual who was not subject to any law whatever. Finally, their empire by necessity reverted to a monarchy, without which it would not have been possible to smother the dissension of ambitious princes, nor to put an end to the countless evils which followed from it. Nevertheless, because of the feebleness and imperfection of the human condition, all of the monarchies mentioned here, just as they had a beginning and period of growth, also suffered decay and finally came to ruin and complete alteration. But many other empires in the past and at present have enjoyed a long duration so long as they were and now are governed and ruled more justly, more equitably, and more virtuously and their leaders are more in accord with the people, the people more in accord with each other and with their leaders. This could never happen unless one among them had maintained his preeminence and his reason according to his estate, and unless the leader was himself ruled by good laws and the customs of society for the common good, to prevent his royal and legitimate power from being transformed into tyranny and willful domination.

Truly, Sire, when I carefully consider the form and manner of the regime which the kings your predecessors have introduced and maintained over the French people, I find it so reasonable and so civilized [*politique*] that it is altogether free from tyranny. That is the reason, in my opinion, why this regime, among all others—Christian as well as infidel—has endured so long and prospered and is now at the height of its glory and prosperity.

For, looking at this French empire as a whole, it partakes of all three forms of political government. First of all, there is the king, who is a monarch altogether loved, obeyed, and revered more than any other one can name (a fact which is widely noted) and who, although he has complete power and authority to command and do whatever he wishes, is nonetheless ruled and limited in the exercise of this great and sovereign liberty by good laws and ordinances and by the multitude and great authority of officials who are so close to him that a king could scarcely act in a way that would be too violent nor work too much to the prejudice of his subjects. And yet, these kings have always had near their persons several princes or other illustrious and notable clerical and lay individuals with whose counsel they have conducted matters of peace and war concerning the state. In this way the kings, by their virtue and valor, provided also that there is good conduct and good counsel of these princes and officials, have accomplished such great deeds in peace and war that, through them they are and will forever be remembered throughout the world. Especially you, Sire, among all the others, as everyone can see.

Touching next the system of justice, we see even there greater orderliness.[3] For there is such a great number of officers, civil and criminal, high administrators as well as subalterns, that a man can scarcely be oppressed and not receive swift reparation if he pursues it. But particularly to be prized are the sovereign courts—both those of the Great Council which attend the king and the Parlements which are located in the various provinces of the kingdom—because the kings your predecessors and you above all others have given them so much authority and favored them with so much reverence in the matter of justice that, when even royalty have been condemned in the courts, they have submitted to the imposition of punishment. As a result, there is not now either so great a prince or so presumptuous a subject who does not fear to disobey the courts. For they are composed of so great a number of good and notable individuals that they are a true Roman senate, representing a majesty which is helpful to the good and dreadful to the bad. Because, particularly, the courts have cognizance, without appeal in the last resort, not only over all civil and criminal matters, but also over all ordinances concerning the interests of parties, over royal letters (even of reprieve and remission), to judge the legality or illegality of such letters and to order fair reparation to injured parties according to their own opinion and mitigation. Hence it occurs that few people, even those who might have something to lose by not acting, would dare do something worthy of punishment, even at the hasty command of a willful prince, because such a command would not excuse them from being punished afterward, whether soon or late, when the exercise of justice would again be given full liberty. This we have seen daily in your times, Sire, when several people have been brought to punishment for violence they or

3. Cf. Seyssel, *The Monarchy of France*, pt. 2, esp. chap. 3 et seq. and chap. 15 et seq.

their predecessors committed during time of war or other times when justice did not have an entirely free rein.

There are, in addition to those already mentioned, other officials who protect the domain of the kings, who take an oath never to allow anything to harm it, no matter what letters or commands to the contrary they may receive. All these institutions have the effect of severely bridling[4] the disorderly will of a willful prince. Thus, in the course of time, before the prince is able to resort to force in order to have his way, it is inevitable that means will be found to make him change his mind or hinder him. Nevertheless, if on occasion some irreparable action has been taken, at a later time some suitable remedy has always presented itself. At the very least, bad ministers (without whom bad princes could scarcely accomplish anything) have been punished in such a way as to serve as a lesson for those who have come after them. This method of procedure is so well and anciently preserved in your kingdom that a prince, no matter how unhampered he may be, would be ashamed to trample it, and many of his subjects and servants would fear counseling or applauding such an action. Thus it follows from what has already been said that sovereign royal power is regulated and moderated by honorable and reasonable means which the kings themselves have introduced and most often protected—you, Sire, above all others of which there is memory, for which reason your Royal Majesty is more acclaimed, more beloved, and better obeyed than those who have resorted to disorderly willfulness.

Next, the second estate of France, the nobility, is well respected and enjoys many benefits and preeminences, as reason dictates, because they are the ones who defend the rest of the population from danger to their lives. Chief among the nobility are the great princes, those of the royal blood as well

4. Ibid., pt. 1, chap. 8.

as some others, who are honored and revered by all subjects
in the same degree as the direct and collateral members of the
royalty. Thus, they command obedience and exercise justice
over all the great estates, peoples, and regions, but are
nevertheless dependent on the monarch and answerable in
the last resort to his sovereign courts. Moreover, several of
these princes are principal members of the Parlement of
Paris, which is the oldest and most respected of the courts.
They also enjoy several other preeminences on account of
their high rank—which is called peerage—which causes
them to be exalted and honored above all other members of
the nobility, much like the cardinals in the estate of the
clergy.

Honored next in rank beneath the princes are the rest of
the nobility. Besides their freedom from all *tailles* and other
such impositions, the nobility is granted many of the great
estates, fiefs, and lordships of the kingdom. They also hold
many high offices and responsibilities for warfare—which is
their principal activity—and for civil order* in many places.
Indeed, the kings honor the nobility so highly and have such
confidence in them that they seem to be royal servants. These
noblemen have the right to carry arms in the king's presence
and to approach the king without suffering the least suspicion. Nonetheless, this second estate of nobility, which is
honored and revered by the people and which enjoys so
much authority over those of the lowest estate, is in such fear
of the system of justice that it has neither law nor strength to
do any evil or act contrary to reason and against those immediately dependent on them.

This is especially true in your reign, Sire, who have so
often reprimanded the audacity of those who wished to oppress the people, the third estate, which has been equally
protected in its liberty by justice in order to trade, labor, and
carry on other activities appropriate to it as a whole and by
which the kingdom is maintained and enriched in general
and in particular. And if the third estate bears the burden of

taxes, it is also the case that it is shielded, defended, and sustained by the nobility against all threats of violence and oppression by neighbors, and by the king and the system of justice against the insolence of the nobility. Moreover, the third estate shares in several of the great honors and emoluments which are common to the nobles and the rest of society, namely, benefices, be they high positions or otherwise. This is the case because those of the third estate, applying themselves more to learning than the nobility, are more likely to be deserving of such responsibilities and thus obtain them by election or by some other means. In addition, the third estate holds most of the judicial offices through which many of that class have attained great wealth and honors. The same is true for offices of finance, accounts, secretaryships, and innumerable others which are available throughout the kingdom and which are not commonly held by members of the nobility.

Thus, the goods and honors, responsibilities and administration of the public weal being divided and parceled out in this manner among all the estates proportionately, according to their condition and preeminence and the equality of each maintained, there ensues a harmony and consonance which is the cause of the preservation and augmentation of the monarchy. And the more the affairs of the kingdom continue to prosper, the kings (who are the fountain and source from which flow and emanate all streams of good policy and justice) are so much the more attentive to maintain this union and correspondence, as true and natural princes who strive primarily for the common good of the kingdom, a good which they consider their own. And this is what we see at present under your most glorious and happy reign; much more, in my opinion, than one can see in any other reign since the beginning of this monarchy (as I believe I have clearly shown in another tract)[5] and of which we can hope to

5. See introduction, n. 22, *Les louenges.*

see even more with the aid of Him on whom all power and authority depends and Who said through the mouth of the prophet, "Through me kings reign and the powerful administer justice." [6]

And as all things are better known and more highly esteemed by comparison and examples than by reason and arguments, it has seemed to me that, passing over all the other empires which have existed, it is advisable to take for comparison only that of the Romans who, without any argument and according to the common judgment of those who have written since that time, be they Greeks or Latins, were for a long time the best and best governed of all the others, either before or after them.

Nevertheless, upon reviewing the beginning and progress of the Roman Empire, one finds that it was never so well ruled nor so justly and equitably governed as that of the French. It was continually vexed and tormented by internal dissensions and by civil strife as long as it was ruled by the many. As a result of these disturbances the military discipline that had been the principal instrument of their growth dissolved, all their other good laws and institutions were thrown into confusion, and their empire finally returned to a government by one man. That government, eventually falling into the hands of tyrannical and feeble-minded princes and they not having their power restrained in the manner already discussed, in the course of time was reduced to the condition which we now see.

And because among all the others who have written on this subject, both Greeks and Latins, Appian the Alexandrian stands out as the one who has provided the most full and detailed knowledge of all their deeds—both good and bad—but above all of their dissensions, seditions, and intestine and civil wars, I thought, Sire, that you would find a

6. Prov. 8:15.

French translation of his history most pleasant because of the natural desire you have always had to know and understand those histories which are not only engaging and attractive to read but which—more to the point—offer some teaching and direction for the just governance and the conduct of affairs of the kingdom as well as the other great countries, lands, provinces, and estates which God in His eternal providence has given to you to rule.

In order to translate this history, which contains so many things worth knowing by all important people, I have exercised extreme diligence to recover all that is available in Latin that represents even the smallest bit of what he wrote. For of the twenty-two[7] books which he mentions in his introduction, only eleven are extant, and not all of them in their entirety, to wit: the books on Lybia, Syria, Parthia, Mithradates, Illyria, the Celts, and five books on the Civil Wars which were translated by Publius Candidus[8] during the reign of Pope Nicholas V of good memory. Among these eleven extant books, only seven have been put into print, to wit: the five on the Civil Wars, the book on Illyria, and the book on the Celts, which is available only in an abridged form. The other four I found as manuscripts in your library. In addition, I have had great difficulty in translating from Latin because of the first translator, who did not have a complete knowledge or understanding of Greek and therefore did not understand in several passages either the meaning of words or the substance of some of the sentences, and who rendered the text in language so obscure and irrelevant in so many places that I can extract no good sense from it. Thus I have been forced from the beginning to guess in places, which is a dangerous and uncertain practice in translation.

7. Twenty-four books are extant.
8. Pier Candido Decembrio (1392–1477), appointed *magister brevium* by Pope Nicholas V in 1450.

However, since having recovered, through your agency, the Greek versions of those eleven books of the history that are available—and which were sent to you by the signoria of Florence—I have once again reviewed and corrected what I have done all along, with the aid of Messire Jean Lascaris,[9] who is a great expert in many languages, and I have found my work so clear, and so well expressed that there is no obscurity nor difficulty whatever. But this has been almost as much trouble for me as doing two translations, because there were so many errors in the Latin.

However, that this history might be easier to read, I have divided and distinguished the books, which were continuous, into several chapters according to the diversity of material and subjects, so that the work as a whole will now, in my opinion, be rather easy to understand and rather delightful and pleasant to read. Thus, the reading of this book will be able to be of profit to your most noble successors and to all other princes, lords, and administrators of kingdoms and provinces, because they will find in it and will see clearly how many detestable and execrable evils have arisen from the ambition of those who wished to rise above others, against reason, in the popular and in the aristocratic state. They will see too in what danger are princes and monarchs who wish to dominate and command their subjects beyond reason and who try more to hold them in servile fear by ambitious and tyrannical domination than to win their filial obedience by paternal love, justice and fair treatment. In addition, private citizens, your subjects, even those Italians recently conquered by you and reduced to obedience to you, will be able to know and judge how much better, more tolerable and desirable, is the empire of a good king and natural prince than of a tyrannical usurper or a commune and assembly of the many. Beyond that, seeing the infinite evils and inestimable damage already suffered by a people who,

9. See introduction, n. 18.

by armed violence and by war, were conquered and subjugated, and even more by those obedient subjects who fell under the power and subjugation of ambitious leaders and factions, the Italians and others now subject to you will count themselves happy to have fallen into your hands and will recognize the mildness and agreeableness of domination by the French. For although you conquered them by force of arms and by the exploits of a most fierce war,[10] you have nevertheless never tried to plunder nor divide their lands or cities among your soldiers, nor impose on them new and unaccustomed penalties or tributes. Rather, you have tried to protect them from all pillage by warriors and others; to preserve and protect their lands and homes by the exercise of justice and orderly rule; and to relieve them from taxes and tributes that they formerly suffered under the domination of tyrants. And, what is even more to be praised and is worthy of perpetual memory, to those who, being thus humanely treated, rebelled against you (as a result of bad counsel and the persuasions of a few hateful and seditious partisans) and were again reduced to your will by force and prowess of arms, you extended so much humaneness and clemency that one could barely perceive that you might have had any anger toward them. Thus, if some punishment has been imposed on them (which was indeed a small price for their misdeed) it has been rather to create fear of any future evil deeds than to correct the one already done. And even that you did with regret. In this manner you have won in the eyes of God, as one must believe, infinite merit; and from men immortal glory, and even more, the heart, the love, and the true obedience of those whom you have subjugated, who will always be the cause of future prosperity and victories, to the praise of God, the augmentation of His Christian religion and the perpetual glory of you and the French nation.

10. Reference to the battle of Agnadello, April 1509; and cf. introduction, n. 22, *La Victoire*.

"Police" and Its Usage

Page	Line	French Form	Page	Line	French Form
35	20	polices	106	29	police
36	15	politié	121	18	police
36	17	police	123	27	police
39	16	policié	124	8	police
41	1	police	128	2	police
41	18	police	128	19	police
43	7	policié	128	23	police
46	8	policié	129	4	police
50	7	policié	129	6	police
50	9	police	129	11	police
51	17	police	149	8	police
56	6	police	149	14	police
65	27	police	149	22	police
67	3	La police	149	24	police
68	7	la police	150	22	police
68	11	police	151	2	police
71	22	police	153	4	police
74	10	police	156	10	police
81	25	police	156	19	police
93	30	police	156	20	police
93	32	police	156	25	police
94	20	police	156	28	police
101	14	police	176	19	police
106	26	la police			

Index